In The Eye Of The Storm

Reengineering Corporate Culture

John R. Childress

Larry E. Senn

The
Leadership
Press

LOS ANGELES • NEW YORK

A Leadership Press book, published by arrangement with the authors.

The
Leadership
Press

LOS ANGELES • NEW YORK

Library of Congress Catalog Card Number: 95-79141

Childress, John R.

In the Eye of the Storm: Reengineering Corporate Culture

Includes index.

1. Corporate Culture. 2. Culture Change. 3. Reengineering.
4. Change Initiatives. 5. Change Management. 6. High-Performance Culture.
I. Senn, Larry E. II. Childress, John R. III. Title.
IV. Title: In the Eye of the Storm: Reengineering Corporate Culture

ISBN 0-9648466-0-8 (hard cover)

Second printing, February 1996

Printed in the United States of America

printing number
2 3 4 5 6 7 8 9 0

Copies of *In the Eye of the Storm: Reengineering Corporate Culture* are available at special discounts for
bulk purchases by corporations, institutions, and other organizations.

Please see the back of the book for an order form, or, for more information, please call:

The Leadership Press, Inc.
3780 Kilroy Airport Way, Suite 800
Long Beach, CA 90806
(800) 788-3380 Phone
(310) 426-5174 Fax

FOREWORD

Richard L. Measelle
Managing Partner, Arthur Andersen LLP

Reengineering is in vogue. It has become one of the most wide-ly-practiced change mechanisms in global business—and justi-fiably so. The company that decides to reengineer its business processes, in the effort to improve its operations and respond more effectively to customers' needs, is the company that values excellence and is realistic about the sources of profitability. It's the company that bravely embraces change...revolutionary change that often leaves the company uncomfortable with itself and unable to identify the source of that discomfort.

Since the early 1980s, Arthur Andersen has been helping clients around the globe reengineer their business processes. We have undertaken many changes in our organization as well. We've learned—both through our own experience and in the process of advising clients—that one critical success factor in reengineering is often downplayed and even ignored: under-standing and addressing the powerful impact of revolutionary change on people. *In the Eye of the Storm: Reenineering Corpo-rate Culture* helps the reader learn both the nature of reengi-neering's impact and what company leaders can do to manage it to the organization's advantage.

To succeed, reengineering must be executed in support of a vision and viewed as a practical exercise. Its practices must be achieved in the context of the company's culture—the tradi-tions and habits and personality that give the company its identity. No one is better qualified to describe the nature of change wrought by reengineering or the way to ease it into a company's culture than the authors. As the co-founders and Senior Partners of The Senn-Delaney Leadership Consulting Group, Inc., John Childress and Larry Senn lead the oldest and most experienced culture research and enhancement firm in the United States. They have helped me and our organization better understand how we can harness the power of our

TABLE OF CHAPTERS

unique culture in the service of our clients. This includes a key realization: that even in an organization like Arthur Andersen, with deep and strong traditions, practices and beliefs, periodic changes to the culture are crucial to the introduction and success of new initiatives. Through a significant body of work with dozens of world-class organizations, John and Larry have determined how to make this aspect of reengineering a positive experience for executives and employees, on a person-by-person level.

The reader interested in making reengineering work will find *In the Eye of the Storm: Reengineering Corporate Culture* practical, useful and applicable to any business situation. It will change the way you look at reengineering, change and corporate culture.

AUTHOR'S REMARKS: CHARTING A NEW COURSE

It is only in the storm,
that we truly become sailors.

The old Chinese saying, "May you live in changing times!" can be either a curse or a blessing, depending on how you look at it. For the past 16 years, we have been blessed with the opportunity to work with several hundred clients, both in the United States and around the globe, all attempting to find new ways to successfully compete in the rapidly changing business world. It seems as if the calm seas of consistency and predictability of previous decades have been replaced by a raging storm, where no organization can escape, or survive, unchanged. Our consulting business is about change; change in strategies, organizational structures, shifts in corporate culture, changes in leadership styles, but also, change in individuals.

The idea for this book—*In the Eye of the Storm*—has come from our years of consulting and more recently from one-on-one dialogues with dozens of CEOs during the writing of a previous book, *21st Century Leadership—Dialogues with 100 Top Leaders*. The majority of the interviews were conducted by our co-author, Lynne Joy McFarland. At first it seemed like a non sequitur to put the words Reengineering and Corporate Culture together. In many people's minds they are separate elements of the business equation. Reengineering is the "hard" side, filled with technical skills, analysis, redesign and, in most cases, layoffs and job-loss, all for the purpose of improved customer service and increased shareholder values. On the other side, corporate culture brings to mind the "softer" side of business, that "vision-thing," shared values, behavior change, mission statements, and teambuilding.

How do these seeming opposites fit together? Because they have to! Each without the other is insufficient for lasting and significant change or improvement. Reengineering without heart can be brutal and create more problems than it cures. Culture Change without new business systems and procedures

can be a useful set of experiences and seminars, but will not ensure fundamental change. Together, in the right mix, with the right skills, they can truly bring about the "radical and fundamental improvements" that are necessary for continued business success in today's highly competitive and rapidly changing global marketplace. It is through the interrelation of these two key elements that businesses can truly find the "eye of the storm!"

This book has been a labor of love. The labor coming from writing a book, actively consulting on client engagements, and leading a growing consulting firm as Co-Managing Partners, all at the same time. The love comes from the work we do; working with CEOs, senior executive teams, middle managers, supervisors and hourly employees to fulfill a shared Vision of "Making a Difference Through Leadership." When you can simultaneously make a difference in the lives of individuals, the effectiveness of teams, and the spirit and performance of organizations, what could be more fulfilling?

Over the past two decades that we have been learning about corporate culture, change management, leadership development, performance improvement and reengineering, we have been personally moved and changed by the very nature of the work we do. To work with individuals who are struggling with difficult business (and sometimes personal) issues, to listen to their "visions," their hopes and fears, hear their concerns for their employees, their belief in their product and the desire to satisfy their customers has been humbling and, at the same time, exhilarating. Nowhere can one be simultaneously more humbled and uplifted than during the processes of reengineering and shifting corporate culture.

Like both reengineering and culture change, this book has been the work of many people; Larry and I were more the "guides" (or Process-Owners in the business vernacular) than authors. In more ways than can be described, the team of consultants and staff of the Senn-Delaney Leadership Consulting Group, Inc. have both supported our writing, challenged and built upon our vague ideas, given us examples from their consulting engagements, read through countless drafts and offered significant suggestions. Bernadette Senn, Scott Tempel and Deirdre Schumacher even rewrote a few of the chapters when

Larry or I had significant "brain spasms" and the words just wouldn't come. Many consultants offered useful input, including: Joe Doyle, Paul Walker, Ernie Webb, John Clayton and Bob Carroll. Joyce Wycoff, an excellent writer, helped with the early efforts to establish the style of this book and did some important research for us, and Peter Brown designed a compelling book jacket cover.

Our clients (all of whom we count as "friends" in many ways) have opened their organizations to our probing and offered up examples of the "good, bad, and the spectacular" from their experiences with reengineering, leadership issues and culture change. Most notable among these have been John P. DesBarres and Nick Neuhausel of Transco Energy Company; Ron Burns of Union Pacific; John Croom and the executives at the Columbia Gas System; and Ray Smith, John Gamba and Brenda Morris at Bell Atlantic Corporation.

We have also benefited greatly from the assistance of Arthur Andersen LLP, who are experts on the reengineering side of the equation and collaborated with us in our efforts to marry the concepts of reengineering and culture change. Our consulting work and professional discussions with Dick Measelle, Jerry Moffatt and other Partners and consultants of Arthur Andersen LLP, have been incredibly helpful. We have drawn on their reengineering expertise and the organizational change efforts of their Business Consulting Group for models and case studies. Without their generosity and commitment to client improvements this book would not have been possible.

We especially want to thank Dick Love who heads the reengineering efforts at Hewlett-Packard for reviewing our first draft and providing some valuable suggestions.

Many of our associations with other firms are opportunities for us to continue to grow, and none has been more impactful than our work with George and Linda Pransky of Pransky & Associates, located in LaConner, Washington. Their work on the Psychology of Mind is expressed in Chapters 8 and 11 as we explore "states of mind," "moods" and "assuming innocence in others." They help us to walk each day with grace and ease, regardless of what challenges are thrown our way.

When is a book ever finished? When is reengineering or culture change ever finished? They're all really "works in

progress." Both these processes are heuristic; loosely meaning that one learns more about the process as one goes through the process. "Learn as you go" is the best phrase for this book, too. Hopefully the Reader Activities will be a jump-start for you the reader, or any leaders wanting to truly make a difference in their organization.

Our sincere desire is that this book and the ideas and examples contained in it will be of value to business leaders as you work at improving the lives of your employees, the effectiveness of internal teams, and the spirit and performance of your organizations. With these ideas put into practice, we have the best shot ever at creating the ultimate win-win-win situation; for all employees, customers, and shareholders!

May you find the "eye of the storm!"

John R. Childress and Larry E. Senn

INTRODUCTION: A STORM IS RAGING

"If you're not confused, you haven't been paying attention!"

A Storm is Raging in Business Today

Beginning in the early 1980s, the rapid rate of technological change, the increase in global competition, and the break from authority-centered work and social environments has heaped one massive set of changes upon another, to brew a gale force storm over traditional business activities. Everywhere organizations are struggling to maintain the viability of their enterprises. Peter Drucker, noted management researcher and author, has perhaps best captured the essence of what is happening in business today:

> *"We are in one of those great historical periods that occur every 200 to 300 years when people don't understand the world anymore, and the past is not sufficient to explain the future."*

One of the key realizations of this past decade of turmoil is that the high rate of change will probably be with us for a long time. There are no "kinder and gentler times" just over the horizon or around the corner. We are going to have to live with change, in our organizations and in ourselves.

However, it may be possible, with the right tools and effective leadership, to find the "eye of the storm," where the organization can capitalize on change, rather that be buffeted about by it. Where a proactive strategy of change can lead to competitive success over those companies merely reacting to change and trying to stay afloat. Where individuals can find balance and fulfillment in their professional and personal lives.

New "tools for change" have arisen to help our businesses successfully navigate through the storm. One of the most important and far-reaching tools for change is Business Process Improvement, or Reengineering.

Reengineering is the word of the day in corporate America. Books, articles, workshops, conferences and lectures herald reengineering...the radical redesign and fundamental rethinking of business processes to achieve dramatic improvements...as the answer to revitalizing our businesses and organizations. And, rightly so. Reengineering can blast through layers of bureaucracy, deadwood, and non-value adding processes. The results are often staggering...processes that once took days, weeks or even months are reduced to hours or sometimes minutes. Costs are often slashed to previously inconceivable levels while service and quality increases dramatically.

Reengineering is more than a buzz-word, it's a fundamental approach...a "clean sheet" way of looking at business processes. Reengineering removes long-standing assumptions, moves past turf issues and uses a customer focus to pull an organization into a new future with extraordinary gains in customer service, speed, productivity and profitability.

That's the good news. And, it's actually great news. Union Carbide lowered fixed costs by $400 million in just three years. Taco Bell experienced a 31% profit growth following reengineering, in spite of massive capital investments made to upgrade technology and facilities. GTE estimates a 30% improvement in productivity resulted from its reengineering efforts. And those are just a few of the many companies that have dramatically improved their performance through reengineering.

There is bad news, however. And the bad news is that a large percentage of all reengineering efforts fail and most extract more of a human price than necessary.

Michael Hammer & James Champy state in their groundbreaking book, *Reengineering the Corporation:*

"Many companies that begin reengineering don't succeed at it. They end their efforts precisely where they began, making no significant changes, achieving no major performance improvement, and fueling employee cynicism with yet another ineffective business improvement program."

The misuse of reengineering has added to its mixed results. Arbitrary downsizings without thoughtful process redesign have increased management workloads and stress levels. Mechanical approaches without adequate communication, training and education have eroded trust and loyalty at all levels.

Why do some organizations succeed while others spend enormous time, energy and money without gaining any noticeable performance improvements? Why is reengineering becoming a negative word when what it can do is sorely needed by companies to compete and in some cases, survive?

We believe the answer is clear. Most reengineering efforts, true to their name, focus on the technical tasks of business processes. What they too often ignore or at best give lip service to is the human side—the behavioral side of change. Anyone who has ever attempted to implement a change of any kind has experienced the phenomenon of resistance to change by people and institutions.

Such was our experience in our early history as performance improvement consultants. Senn-Delaney Associates began as an engineering-based performance improvement consulting firm in the late 1960s. We found through our early experiences with clients that:

It was easier to decide on change than to get people to change!

People and organizations are creatures of habit and changing habits is much harder than changing structures or systems. It seemed to us that organizations, like people, had personalities and to ignore or not deal with an organization's personality traits could be fatal to our change efforts. Today people recognize that aspect of organizations as Corporate Culture and the business world is slowly beginning to appreciate the power of cultural habits.

Our early experiences led us to found The Senn-Delaney Leadership Consulting Group, devoted solely to reshaping or "reengineering" corporate culture to support business change initiatives. Since 1978, Senn-Delaney Leadership has helped corporate clients with the change management aspects of restructuring, strategy development and implementation, mergers and acquisitions, reengineering, customer service initiatives, and total quality programs.

Through all these activities, there was one constant that determined the level of success or failure—the corporate culture.

We have long known that the only way to ensure maximum success at any broad-based change initiative is to systematically deal with the corporate culture.

To truly reengineer the corporation, you need to reengineer the culture.

It is also interesting to note that James Champy, in a sequel, *Reengineering Management*, states:

"Everything we've learned about reengineering drives toward one solid conclusion: The rules of governance (and self-governance) for effective business enterprises today are being determined by their culture, not their organizational structure."

The thoughts and ideas developed in this book are designed to ensure that your reengineering, restructuring or other performance improvement efforts have the greatest probability of success.

To accomplish this, we are focusing on how leadership and culture change can positively impact and influence the reengineering process. Many of the examples and case studies presented throughout this book are drawn from our clients and consulting experiences in dealing with the role of culture in performance improvement.

"Finding the Eye": Bell Atlantic

"Bell Atlantic is a reengineering success story...a much touted hero that slashed service installation time from 16 days to 8 hours and has begun to win back customers from alternate-access carriers."

One of the best examples of the change in culture required for successful reengineering comes from our work with the Bell

Atlantic Corporation. Their reengineering processes have been written about extensively, but we think the interesting part of their story happened before they began their reengineering efforts.

Before the breakup of AT&T in 1984, the culture of the Bell System was a classic example of how a corporate culture can evolve to successfully compliment the strategies and organizational structures of a company. Because the Bell System developed and flourished in a highly regulated, monopolistic environment, their corporate culture adapted to meet those conditions. The old Bell culture was highly structured and bureaucratic with lifetime employment as the "social contract" between company and employees. Also, being the only game in town had created an atmosphere which was far from customer-driven, although they were highly focused on customer service, as *they* defined it. To standardize procedures and ensure reliable telephone service, a book of practices and procedures (known as "BST" or "the Practice") was created and followed religiously by employees as they responded to business or customer problems. In fact, if it wasn't in the "BST", it simply wasn't done.

While in today's highly competitive world that situation sounds like a "design to fail," we must remember that it was a regulated monopoly and this was the culture that best fit that environment. As a result, the United States had the finest, most reliable and ubiquitous telephone service in the world.

When divestiture was decreed, Bell Atlantic became one of the new "Baby Bells" created by the break-up of AT&T. At that time, Bell Atlantic had a vigorous Management-by-Objective (MBO) system in place. While that system worked well for the monopolistic system, it didn't work well at all for a young company that suddenly needed to be more flexible, innovative, competitive and customer-driven. Ray Smith, the CEO who leads Bell Atlantic's ongoing transformation process, states,

> *"As long as resources are easy to get, competition minor, and business moves at a fairly predictable pace, the MBO system works. But the moment individuals must take initiatives in their own departments that diminish a departmental objective for the good of the corporation, the MBO system fails."*

Smith took over as the Chairman and CEO of Bell Atlantic in 1989 and immediately recognized that it needed to drastically change its culture while at the same time implementing new competitive strategies. Smith saw three primary areas that needed to change:

- **Individual Accountability**—People were feeling victimized by divestiture, with too much finger pointing and blaming. There were too many excuses and not enough proactive work on improving processes and performance.

- **Turf Issues**—Smith also felt that they operated too much in what he called "stovepipes" (territorial groups that saw themselves as internally competitive rather than mutually supportive). In order to truly compete in a global economy, the "new" Bell Atlantic couldn't act as six or seven separate state organizations or as separate functional areas. They had to become a more unified, effective operation.

- **Bias-for-Action**—It was also clear that no matter what shifts took place to improve the business, that an overall sense-of-urgency needed to be imbedded in all employees. (Things had to get done faster, with fewer committees, less meetings, shorter reviews, lower-level sign-offs, fewer people in the decision cycle, etc.)

Smith began the change process by defining a set of principles he called the Obligations of Leadership. He believed that these principles were the foundation necessary to transform the company into a successful competitor in the rapidly changing Telecommunications and Information industry. While many of the managers agreed with him on the changes needed and the new behaviors defined in the Obligations of Leadership, the change wasn't happening as rapidly as it was needed. Like many other CEOs trying to bring about change, Smith was frustrated by the slow pace of change at Bell Atlantic.

About that time, we had an initial meeting with Ray Smith and shared with him some of our experiences in facilitating corporate culture changes. We struck a chord with him by explaining the importance of giving people a shared emotional experience of his vision for Bell Atlantic and the new cultural values he felt necessary. In order for people to truly understand what he was saying, they had to experience it. Without that experience, the principles would remain abstract concepts.

Being a visionary leader, as well as an accomplished amateur actor and playwright, Smith quickly made the connection between Bell Atlantic and a play. He could easily see that a great play is really only words on paper until the emotion and drama of the cast brings it to life for the audience. In this case, the "cast" was the senior management team and the audience the 80,000-plus employees of Bell Atlantic.

With this new understanding of what was needed, we designed and delivered an executive leadership and culture change process which began with a three-day, off-site, team-building retreat for senior management. This was developed to give them a shared experience of the new culture. The Bell Atlantic officers spent three days in an environment of increased accountability, trust, open communication, feedback, listening, and teamwork. It was just the experience they needed. Just as it's impossible to really understand the culture of a foreign country from reading a book, it's not feasible for people to comprehend a new corporate culture just by talking or reading about it. They have to experience it.

At the end of the retreat, many said "Aha, now we understand what Ray's been talking about!" They decided they wanted everyone to experience this new culture and, to give them a guide, they created The Bell Atlantic Way, which included the values, behaviors, and philosophies they felt were the necessary foundations of the new culture. The Bell Atlantic Way behaviors became the guideline for conducting their business internally and externally. It is their code of conduct, a statement describing their new culture.

THE BELL ATLANTIC WAY BEHAVIORS

Our Responsibilities:

As Bell Atlantic employees, we share the responsibility to fully support our company's vision and the goals and strategies that will take us there. Therefore we must:

▶ **Team Play.** This means that I constantly ask the questions: "Who is Bell Atlantic?" "What is my team's purpose, and does that meet the requirements of customers, employees, shareowners or communities?" Also, I do not foster internal competition. I focus my energy on new ways to create a win for the entire team.

▶ **Accept Accountability**. This means asking: "What more can I do to get the results?" rather than looking for reasons why something did not get done. Accountable people look for ways to get the job done.

▶ **Empower**. I empower people when I trust them to do the job and do it well. I give them the authority and the resources they need to do their best, and I offer support and coaching to help them through.

▶ **Care About and Recognize Others**. This means I truly care about the personal and professional well-being of my colleagues, and I go out of my way to recognize their achievements and make them feel appreciated and valuable.

▶ **Listen and Be Here Now.** This means that when I am with someone, I care about what they have to say. I put other thoughts out of my mind so that I can "Be Here Now" with that person.

▶ **Encourage Risk**. I get outside of the "9 Dots" (outside of my comfort zone) to solve a problem even if I am not sure what the results will be. I show the members of my team that the only way to lose is by not trying to win.

▶ **Focus on Priority Issues**. I prioritize my time so that I take care of my "blue chips" first. I trust other members of my team with those things I don't have time to take care of myself.

Before Bell Atlantic launched its reengineering process, they were creating a new, high-performance culture.

Successful reengineering is about change...being willing to challenge the status quo...the old methods...being open to listen to any kind of idea, not being defensive or protective or insecure, working in groups to make things better, having a big picture focus, and looking at what's best for the whole company rather than just an individual function. Those elements were imbedded in The Bell Atlantic Way and allowed them to create a culture that supported the reengineering process that was introduced later.

Smith recently stated:

> *"Developing a culture of teamwork and accountability...The Bell Atlantic Way...has given us a foundation that allowed our restructuring and reengineering efforts to be successful...and allowed us to become a major player in development of the Information Superhighway."*

"When Do You Want It?" Service

One of Bell Atlantic's early reengineering processes addressed the time it took to connect customers to long-distance carriers. Recognizing that the market was becoming more and more competitive, they realized they couldn't afford to continue in the old way which often took as long as 16 days to complete. Brenda Morris, Director of Reengineering at Bell Atlantic took on the project and began to build a reengineering team...without the benefit of budget or allocated headcount. Morris describes the process:

> *"This was a risk-taking adventure. None of us had ever done this before. **The Bell Atlantic Way** had already been started, so I was looking for people who already demonstrated those behaviors...people who were good team players...empowered people ready to take a risk, people who listened and recognized others...leaders who cast good shadows.*

"I had no budget and no head count. When I found the people who I felt could help the team move ahead quickly, I went to them first and explained the risk. I told them what we were getting ready to do and that it was a risky venture because we've never done it before and we didn't know how well it would go. I told them I wanted them to help blow away the old process and start over. Everyone I talked to wanted to be part of the team, but since I had no budget or head count, I had to go to their bosses. I had to explain to them the importance of the project and ask them to continue to absorb the costs of these people. I asked them to keep the head count and pay all the expenses...and do it indefinitely. Every one of them said 'yes'.

"I don't think I would have gotten that kind of cooperation before we started The Bell Atlantic Way. It was The Bell Atlantic Way and the training that the senior management had gone through that helped me get the best people for this reengineering project even though their home divisions had to continue paying their expenses. That was my first awakening that the culture change was really working. These were truly the best people that their managers were letting go to this new project."

Implementing **The Bell Atlantic Way** created a culture that allowed reengineering to succeed. Within a few months, Brenda Morris' group was able to offer "When do you want it?" service. No longer were customers told when a service could be available; they were asked when they wanted it...and that's when it was delivered. What transpired was a dramatic improvement; hookup time went from 16 days to "when you want it." Developing this level of service required a team effort across many departments and across locations, but it set the standard for the company and quickly became the benchmark for other companies.

REENGINEERING, LEADERSHIP AND CULTURE CHANGE

In this book, we lay out a blueprint for a culture change process that supports reengineering or other performance improvement initiatives. This is not a cosmetic make-over or a repackaging of motivation theories. Changing corporate culture requires a rethinking that is as fundamental as the rethinking required for reengineering. It requires a shift in our understanding of people and the people-side of organizational performance. It stretches and reformulates our paradigms of leadership.

Fortunately you don't have to start over with new employees to create a new culture, but it does require a sincere willingness to look at management skills, leadership styles, reward systems and the behavior of people at all levels of the organization.

Many people today are emphasizing the negatives of our current business situation within this country...the loss of jobs, the imbalanced trade level, the massive deficit, poor quality and the seeming loss of motivation in the American worker. We believe this is an example of seeing the glass as half-empty rather than half-full! We believe that today's business organizations have an incredible level of potential inherent in them and that reengineering is a powerful tool for releasing that potential. Before this tool can be used, however, it must be plugged in to a power source. The power source is the people in the organization and their collective values, beliefs and norms...what is commonly called the corporate culture.

Once this source of power is energized and aligned with the organization's vision and goals, phenomenal improvements in performance become almost routine. The following chapters will show you how to harness the incredible power of corporate culture and use it to supercharge all your performance improvement efforts.

1

REENGINEERING: AN OPPORTUNITY FOR REAL CHANGE

Pepsi	Pricing errors reduced 95%.
Federal Mogul	Sample development process shortened from 20 weeks to 18 days.
GTE	Problems solved on first call improved from .5% to 70%.
Macy's	Assortment-related non-purchase rate cut from 56% to 29%.
American Express	$1 Billion slashed from annual expenses and a new product created.

There comes a time for every organization when getting better isn't good enough, when continuous improvement doesn't keep pace with the changes in the marketplace...a time when a breakthrough is required. Many organizations today are achieving that leap through reengineering. The companies listed above are just a few that have achieved the startling improvements that often result from reengineering.

CSC Index, Inc. did a study of 20 recent cases of successful reengineering and found that cost reductions averaged 56%, quality improved an average of 73% and cycle time was reduced an average of 80%. Phenomenal results, often in an amazingly short period of time. Years, and often decades, of accumulated corporate fat—inefficiencies, redundancies, and misdirected efforts—are surgically removed leaving a leaner, more effective organization.

Most managers find it hard to believe that their organizations could possibly have so much inefficiency built into their systems. After all, many of them have had Total Quality Management, Customer Service, or other performance improvement programs in place for years. However, in a world with an ever-escalating rate of change, Total Quality, with its focus on continuous improvement, may not be fast enough or broad enough to assure survival. It's like a car trying to catch a jet...no matter how great the car or how hard we push the accelerator, we're never going to catch-up. Periodically we have to break through to a new level of efficiency or we will be left hopelessly behind.

This breakthrough requires a clean sheet mentality. Everything connected to the old ways must be subordinated to the effort to find a better way. Organizations must be willing to throw out procedure manuals, retire equipment before it's depreciated, burn their organization charts and look at business processes through the eyes of its customers. Not an easy task but the rewards are enormous.

FEDERAL MOGUL CORPORATION

Federal Mogul is an auto parts manufacturer that makes bearings, crankcase covers, oil seals, etc. When an auto manufacturer has a new part that needs to be made, they give the specifications to Federal Mogul and its competitors. Each of the competitors develop a sample part that the auto manufacturer tests and uses to make the final purchase decision.

When Federal Mogul began its reengineering process, development time for sample parts averaged 20 weeks. The best competitors in the industry could turn out a sample product in six weeks. This was a problem for Federal Mogul, although not because the auto manufacturers gave the job to the first company that delivered a functioning sample. Auto manufacturers would wait to decide on a vendor until all the samples were submitted. However, a company that could produce a sample in six weeks had an extra 14 weeks to get customer feedback and refine its product. Some competitors had three chances to get it right before Federal even crossed the line with its first sample. Not surprisingly, Federal Mogul's win rate had fallen to 18%!

Federal Mogul's old system is an example of how processes slowly, with seeming logic, grow inefficient. The old way was for a sales rep to call on a customer and get specifications for a new part. Those specifications were given to engineering (in Detroit) who would create the design at the CAD/CAM terminal and mail it to a manufacturing plant which had available manu-facturing capacity (generally in Ohio). At that plant, the design would go into the tool room where the tools would be cut and returned to the manufacturing floor to actually make the part.

While this sounds like a reasonably logical system, in a world where time is a significant element of added-value, it was a five-month nightmare. The first problem was specifica-tion errors—salespeople took the specifications from the cus-tomers (sometimes informally over lunch or on a cocktail napkin) and delivered them to the design engineers...a two hand-off process that invited many mistakes. The new system corrected this by creating a sales and engineering team to call on customers and develop specifications.

The next major area of lost time was in the design process, which used an inefficient technology that started from scratch on every project. This was replaced by new technology which incorporated a database of every part and tool designed in the past. With the new technology, engineers could quickly check the database for similar designs, change dimensions and have a new design almost immediately. Design processes that once took a week or more could now be done in minutes.

Rather than trusting designs to the mail or delivery systems which added another day or two to the process, Federal linked all the players together with an e-mail system that allowed immediate transfer of the design to any facility. However, actu-al tooling and manufacturing remained the biggest areas of lost time in the old system, based on two primary problems:

- tool rooms were "owned" by the manufacturing plant and a plant selected for its available manufacturing capacity might be backlogged in the tooling area; and

- sample manufacturing was perceived as a nuisance by plant managers who had to disrupt their normal manufacturing flow to produce the one-unit run.

These problems were eliminated, first by creating a "virtual tool room" for the company. Tool rooms were no longer owned by any plant and all were available for any project that needed to be done. Tools would be cut and then trucked to the plants where they were needed. The second major change was to make everyone aware of the importance of the sample development process. Fred Musone, President of Federal Mogul told people,

> *"You are not to think of yourselves as salespeople, engineers or manufacturing people...you are business people first with a common concern, a common goal and a common objective.*

> *"When I told our people that they were business people who needed to use their expertise for the good of the total enterprise, I was just asking them to pay attention to where value is created and what our customers pay us for.*

> *"You've got to understand your focus...and it's not finance or manufacturing or distribution or R&D. That's why we have to have a global measure called the enterprise and why people have to be business people first. If you're in finance or sales or design or MIS or R&D, you'd better be doing things that give velocity to our processes...not the reverse.*

> *"One example of functional thinking we ran into as we got started was a factory that had components available for assembly. We could see the parts but we could not go get them and put them into the assembly process because the system had not released the material. We're not here for the system...the system is here for us. That's why we have to subordinate our functional responsibilities to the needs of the enterprise."*

As Federal's plant managers switched from a concern only for manufacturing to a commitment to the success of the entire business operation, they were increasingly willing to give sample development its proper priority.

Results for Federal Mogul have been impressive. Sample development cycle time was cut from 20 weeks to 18 days... and the win rate improved from 18% to 80%! Inventory was cut in half and the bottom line more than doubled as the company increased sales from $698 million to just over $1 billion in four years.

Pepsi's "10X"—Breakthrough Thinking

In the early 90s, Pepsi was feeling the impact of alternative beverages such as bottled ice tea which were absorbing almost all the growth in the industry. The battle was no longer between Coke and Pepsi. In an era of mass-tailoring there were hundreds of soft-drink options for consumers to choose from. Snapple, Perrier and Hansen's had become household names at the expense of the cola-market.

Pepsi launched a corporate-wide reengineering effort under the banner "10X"—short hand for the mission of achieving a ten times improvement in speed, cost and quality. This huge undertaking was marketed with all the pizzazz of a new product launch, complete with logos, slogans, professional graphics and T-shirts.

One of the operations reengineered was customer order fulfillment. As Pepsi looked at processes that had evolved to handle customer orders, they found redundancies, wasted time and systems that led to inaccuracies. They had six customer databases, with approximately 60% of the information being obsolete. Up to 40% of the invoices contained errors and some customers received as many as six billing statements. Many accounts had three separate salespeople and delivery trucks calling on them and some trucks returned at the end of the day still carrying up to 50% of their original load. Stock-outs were frequent, about 20% of customer accounts were not serviced regularly and customer representatives spent up to two hours per day doing administrative paper work.

Pepsi realized that customer order fulfillment was an interlocking series of subprocesses, which they labeled "The Customer Chain," including setting up customer information, making the sale and capturing order information, making product available, delivering the product and preparing an invoice.

Information technology was added to the chain in the form of a new hand-held terminal for customer reps. The device automated pricing information and gave the reps the ability to offer price discounts based on accurate performance criteria. The hand-held continuously reconciles delivery routes during the day and generates end-of-the-day reports, reducing a rep's administrative time from two hours to about 15 minutes. In addition to giving reps extra time to sell and service accounts, the hand-helds generated a 95% reduction in pricing/deal errors.

Pepsi also implemented a centralized sales force to improve service, increase anticipatory selling, and improve delivery under the banner, "The Products You Want, When You Want Them ... It's That Simple."

By 1994, Pepsi had over 25 reengineering labs going and was completely redesigning its information systems, implementing new job designs for 18,000 employees, redeploying 2,500 employees, and staffing 500 new positions and started a new Customer Service Center.

Janice Montle, who led and designed Pepsi's reengineering effort which involved 85% of its employee base, states,

> *"This was a different approach to change management...we had to reach people where they lived...'Head, Heart and Hands' was our banner. This meant that people needed to understand the 'why' of the change. They needed to embrace and believe in what we were doing. And, they needed the training and the coaching to execute the how. A lot was hitting them at once but the results of our reengineering campaign depended upon our people being motivated and capable of making it happen.*

> *"We launched a continuous campaign of '10X' communication using every media possible...videotapes, town meetings, Q&A bulletins. The most effective communication continued to be the stories that were told by our front-line people who participated in the labs or in the pilot. Their credibility and their passion has unbelievable impact."*

REENGINEERING: FAD OR FACT?

The word is everywhere...magazines, television, newspapers, on the street, in the boardroom. People often use the word as if it were a sophisticated synonym for change. It's not. While it always involves change, it's far more than "just change."

Our broad-based definition of reengineering is:

An organization-wide, radical redesign and fundamental rethinking of business processes, organizational design, and corporate culture, to achieve dramatic improvements in the ability to create and deliver added value to the customer.

Radical redesign. Fundamental rethinking. Business processes. Corporate culture. Dramatic improvements. Added value. As you can see, reengineering is more than just cost cutting or "downsizing." It's more than just a band-aid approach to pricing or budget problems. More than any other business improvement tool, true reengineering is "holistic" in its approach and comprehensive in its activities. Nothing is sacred. Everything is focused on the customer.

Reengineering didn't start with the coining of the term or the publication of Michael Hammer and James Champy's book. It's probably been around forever. Every time someone threw out the old ways and started over in order to achieve a quantum leap, it was basically reengineering. When Montgomery Ward decided to sell products through a National mail-order catalog distribution system, it was a radical redesign of how products were sold. Every catalog after that was an improvement or an attempted improvement. When Federal Express developed an overnight delivery service, it was a fundamental rethinking of a business process that created a new industry. And, when banks began to use automated tellers, they created a dramatic improvement in customer service.

Reengineering isn't just about the mechanical redesign of how products get built or distributed. It's much more than just finding a more efficient way to build a product or deliver a service. We've always been doing that in American business. And it's usually been enough. But not anymore! Global competition, the rapid rate of technological change, and shifting workplace values have put tremendous pressures on once impregnable US businesses. In today's global business environment it's not about just getting better any more, it's about survival.

What's fundamentally different about reengineering is that it looks at the entire business as one system and sees it as a highly interconnected series of processes, not a collection of organizations or departments. Most other performance improvement attempts have focused on pieces of the organization, and usually stayed within one area or department. While these improvements didn't achieve huge savings, they did avoid the biggest headache in an improvement effort: *departmental turf issues and functional ownership arguments*. In other words, "people problems" and "cultural issues" usually kept the improvement efforts fairly localized.

Had it not been for the dramatic impact of foreign competition and quantum technological leaps, American businesses would have probably taken the incremental improvement approach for a long time. Continuing in the familiar manner would not have been particularly dramatic, but it would have been easier than running headlong into the corporate culture, turf-issues, or command-and-control leadership styles that tended to perpetuate themselves. Reengineering sees functionalization and command-and-control corporate cultures as "the enemy," which, if eliminated, would lead to some fairly logical and dramatic performance improvements.

The time is right for reengineering and all the tools and learning necessary are now in place. In essence, reengineering has come about as a blending of some essential tools and organizational understanding, including:

- Intense competitive pressures that shifted the game plan from improvement to survival
- Industrial process improvement practices
- Japanese-inspired total quality concepts and tools
- Rapid technological advances leading to real-time communications and information availability
- The shift from individual performance to high-performance work teams
- Understanding and acceptance of the power of corporate culture
- Shifts in individual accountability, and the value of empowerment
- New definitions of leadership for the 21st Century

Reengineering and TQM

There is a good deal of discussion about the relationship of reengineering to Total Quality Management. Is reengineering really just TQM redefined? Is there a difference and does it really matter? Michael Hammer has a nice way of relating the two that shows the importance of both.

> *"We always need TQM...it's like a nice upward slope on a graph...continuously getting better, making incremental improvements. Every once in a while however, slow steady change is not enough. We have to break the mold and start over. Auto makers could have improved the standard-shift transmission forever, but fundamentally rethinking the process from the eyes of their customers told them that most people really didn't want to manually shift gears, hence the automatic transmission. When the same mind-set is applied to business processes, it's reengineering, and it creates quantum leaps in effectiveness and efficiency."*

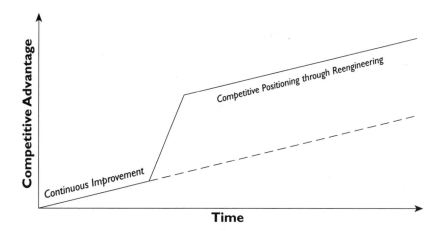

While TQM does focus on work processes, customers and improvements, it tends to do so within a given area or function. Even if it is a broader-based total quality effort, like that of

Xerox in the 1980s, it usually stops short of rebuilding the entire company around the customer. It tends to be applied locally where it can flourish within teams and certain departments. TQM is valuable and many of the elements and concepts of TQM are basic to the process of reengineering. Unfortunately, it doesn't go far enough, or fast enough for today's competitive requirements.

Shifting from Functional to Process Management

The major element of reengineering that distances it from all other improvement efforts is its focus on Process Management instead of Functional Management. Functional Management is a concept that has served a useful purpose in the past, but it is cumbersome and unresponsive to the needs of customers and employees in today's highly competitive and fast changing global business arena. The functional organization is based on a set of concepts that were right for their time: division of labor, standardization of parts and products, mass production, and the need to control, monitor, and oversee work and people. All these useful organizational and business principles allowed companies to grow huge, while still being able to control and manage streams of production and large numbers of people.

The problem with a functional approach to business, however, is the difficulty that comes with imposing order and attempting to tie multiple pieces of the organization together. The result is multiple hand-offs from department to department as work passes through the system. This creates delays, mistakes, bottlenecks, excess supervision, and turf-issues, often slowing the process to a snail's pace. All too often the classic functional organization winds up with additional layers of hierarchy, increased bureaucracy, inflexibility in policies and procedures, and high cost structures with burdensome overhead rates. We even begin setting up departments to check on other departments!

Perhaps with better teamwork and more interpersonal relationship training the functional organizational model could have been made to work. But the world of business has recently taken a dramatic shift due to increased global competition, the rapid rate of change in technology, and shifting social values. And it only seems to be intensifying. (See the book *"21st Century Leadership—Dialogues with 100 Top Leaders"* for an in-depth understanding of the forces shaping business today.)

An additional barrier to the success of Functional Management has also arisen. Functional management is based on the concept of "command-and-control" where those in power tend to organize and oversee those who do the work. While this may have worked well in special situations, like the military, or large factories filled with unskilled workers, today's worker is very different. Shifting social and individual values, more women and minorities at all levels of the job market, combined with easy access to information (information that was once only known at the top of the organization), has lead to a radically different workforce. A workforce that is less willing to work in a hierarchical, command-and-control environment. A workforce that demands more involvement and more fulfillment from work, beyond just a paycheck. A workforce that will change jobs for less pay, but more opportunity. A workforce that is highly diverse in their styles, ideas, abilities, goals, and motivations.

The only real workable solution is to reorganize around processes (or customers) instead of functions. And that is the essence of reengineering. Successful reengineering requires a shift from Functional Organizational Thinking to Process-based Organizational Thinking.

THE MIGRATION FROM FUNCTIONAL TO PROCESS-BASED MANAGEMENT

FUNCTIONAL ORGANIZATION   PROCESS-BASED ORGANIZATION

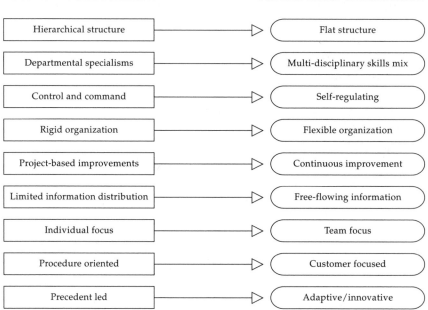

Functional Organization	Process-Based Organization
Hierarchical structure	Flat structure
Departmental specialisms	Multi-disciplinary skills mix
Control and command	Self-regulating
Rigid organization	Flexible organization
Project-based improvements	Continuous improvement
Limited information distribution	Free-flowing information
Individual focus	Team focus
Procedure oriented	Customer focused
Precedent led	Adaptive/innovative

Source: Business Intelligence

But process is everywhere! It's not just localized in the shipping department, the accounts receivable area, or the manufacturing floor. That's functional thinking. If you see things as a process, then you quickly realize that they are all interrelated and to fix one is to fix them all. And to attempt to fix the business process means we must also deal with the people process—corporate culture!

Reengineering cuts across political and functional boundaries to encompass the entire process being redesigned in order to increase total customer value. In a recent article in *Psychology Today*, Tom Peters was quoted as saying that a good deal of organizational stress comes from the fact that we spend 40 percent of our day "saluting." In the realm of reengineering, there is no time for saluting and following bureaucratic "chains of command." Added value to the customer and efficiency of the process are the primary concerns. Reengineering is not about individual egos, empire building, reduction of head count, increasing inventory turns or improving cash flow. It's about focusing on improving customer value and knowing that focus will bring improved financial performance. It's about redefining the way we manage, lead, and interact while at work. It's about a whole new way of serving the customer and providing value.

As Fred Musone at Federal Mogul says,

"You can't make a business better by looking at a balance sheet and you cannot run a business focusing on earnings. Earnings don't cause anything...they are a result of excellence. If you want to make a business better, you'd better focus on what causes earnings. Earnings are the ultimate judge of how well you have created excellence. Sitting in interminable meetings talking about earnings, will not make your business better. The only thing that will make your business better is to exceed the expectations of your customers. And that comes from the value-creating processes. Reengineering an accounts payable process may create a cost savings, but it's not the same thing as reengineering a value-creating process."

2

STORM CLOUDS: THE PROBLEMS ARE BIGGER THAN WE THOUGHT

This reengineering concept sounds great, but…

It's probably just another fad that management will get over soon.

It's just management's way of saying they're going to lay people off.

The last team I was on made a great suggestion and no one listened.

My area's doing fine so why should I get involved?

If I get put on one of those teams, won't I just be reengineering myself out of a job?

I'll never make my bonus if I have to work on one of those time consuming cross-functional teams.

I'm getting hammered on my budget…I don't have time to think about anything else.

If people would just go by the policies, we wouldn't have all these problems.

Who has time for all that Action Team stuff?

The above comments are all too typical as organizations rush into reengineering efforts, hoping to achieve the spectacular improvements touted by the business press. And it is estimated that in 1994 alone, American businesses spent an estimated $32 billion on reengineering, with an estimated growth of 20% per year for the next three years, and a $52 billion outlay by 1997.

With the best intentions, hundreds of companies are embarking on reengineering efforts only to run into brick walls. More often than not their efforts are derailed and reengineering becomes another failed "flavor of the month" improvement process.

Unfortunately, reengineering disappointments are the rule rather than the exception.

According to Michael Hammer, his earlier prediction of nearly a two-thirds failure rate still stands, nearly two years after corporations jumped head-long into reengineering efforts. And the failure rate may be even higher.

A study conducted by Arthur D. Little Inc., reported that only 16% of 350 executives interviewed said they were "fully satisfied" with the results of their reengineering efforts. In fact, 68% of these executives reported that their reengineering efforts created additional problems that were unintended at the beginning of the process (*Informationweek*, June 20, 1994).

REENGINEERING REPORT CARD

North America and Europe (99 companies)

16%	Extraordinary Results	A
17%	Strong Results	B
42%	Mediocre to Marginal	C/D
25%	Failed—No Results	F

Adapted from: State of Reengineering Report: CSC Index, 1994

REASONS FOR FAILURE

There are many reasons for failure. In a recent article titled: *"No Need for Excuses,"* Michael Hammer and Steven Stanton suggest that there are fundamentally two causes for reengineering failure: Failures of Intellect (information and understanding) and Failures in Leadership! They conclude the reason for the large number of reengineering failures lies not in the process of reengineering itself, but in the poor understanding, execution and commitment to the process.

Reengineering didn't fail; they failed to reengineer!

James Champy's book, *Reengineering Management*, delves into one of the biggest reasons that most reengineering efforts fail: outdated and ineffective management practices. Champy points out that work can't be reengineered without first changing the way managers do their jobs. Leadership, teamwork, empowerment, and motivation are what seem to be lacking in today's management tool kit and what is needed to get reengineering on the right path. By talking with several executives who were intimately involved with reengineering and are painfully aware of its difficulties, Champy identified five vital "Core Processes of Management" necessary for reengineering to work:

- Mobilizing the troops behind the initiative
- Enabling the workforce to accomplish the change
- Defining the objectives
- Measuring performance
- Communicating to employees throughout the process

Reengineering is an aggressive, ambitious undertaking requiring a fundamental rethinking of the organization structure, management skills, and the basic processes of how work is carried out. It always involves a broad cross-section of people, shifting the basic concepts of how things get done, and the application of new technology.

McKinsey & Company studied 100 companies undergoing reengineering. Their analysis concluded that five out of six key ingredients for success were cultural and, if given insufficient attention by management, could act as significant barriers to the success of reengineering efforts (Harvard Business Review, Nov.–Dec., 1993).

A study by Deloitte & Touche of 400 US and Canadian companies listed a number of obstacles to business reengineering success. Most are obviously "cultural" in nature.

Obstacles to Business Reengineering Success

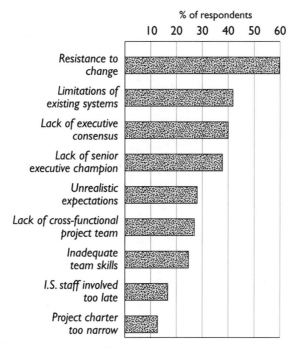

Note: Total exceeds 100% due to multiple answers

Source: Copyright© 1994 by CMP Publications, Inc., 600 Community Drive, Manhasset, NY 11030. Reprinted from INFORMATIONWEEK with permission.
Data: Deloitte & Touche, 1993 Survey of 400 U.S. and Canadian CEOs.

For anyone who has been through a performance improvement effort, it doesn't take studies to prove that "people-issues" are often significant barriers to success.

Unfortunately, corporate leaders all too often underestimate the difficulty of implementing a dramatic shift in performance. The shift from the old ways of doing things to new, untested ways is wrenching and leaves every person involved in a state of uncertainty and confusion. Will the new ways work? What will my role be? Will I be able to handle the new work? Will I have a new boss who will treat me fairly? Will I like my new co-workers? Will I still have my place in the new scheme of things?

Jack Welch of GE, summarizes his thoughts on the difficulty of implementing a major reengineering effort and what is required for success:

> *"When I try to summarize what I've learned since 1981, one of the big lessons is that change has no constituency. People like the status quo. They like the way it was. When you start changing things, the good old days look better and better.*

> *"You've got to be prepared for massive resistance.*

> *"Incremental change doesn't work well in the type of transformation GE has gone through. If your change isn't big enough, revolutionary enough, the bureaucracy can beat you. Look at Winston Churchill and Franklin Roosevelt: They said, This is what it's going to be. And then they did it. Big, bold changes, forcefully articulated. When you get leaders who confuse popularity with leadership, who just nibble away at things, nothing changes. I think that's true in countries and in companies."*

FALSE STARTS: THE NEED FOR PERSISTENCE

Unwavering commitment and a "can-do" attitude are two key cultural traits needed to succeed in reengineering. Many companies have overcome early failures by eliminating cultural barriers. American Express Travel Related Services Co. and Amoco Corp. are cases in point.

American Express' Randy Christofferson, Senior Vice President of Quality and Reengineering, stresses that experience is a better teacher than a written approach or methodology; in other words, "if you make a mistake, spend some more money and try again." For following this advice, the company was rewarded by seeing its corporate annual costs cut by more than $1.2 billion.

One major problem standing in the way of successful reengineering at American Express was a facet of its corporate culture. People tended to join into "camps" or "factions" that then became resistant to other tools or techniques. In this case it was a battle between two camps: TQM versus reengineering. Each had its own faction. "We wallowed in debate," Christofferson reports, about how the two were related and which was more important. Finally, he cut through the disputes and simply redefined reengineering using TQM terminology, enabling American Express to launch 285 reengineering projects that moved the company's credit-card business "closer to the goals of customers, employees and shareholders, slashed costs and wooed back customers and merchants."

Another lesson from the American Express experience is to be realistic about timelines for completing reengineering projects. "Early on American Express believed that reengineering projects could be completed in six months or less, however, most actually took up to two years."

Amoco Corp. twice tried and failed at reengineering. The third attempt, which took 15 months beginning in June 1992, proved the charm, and allowed Amoco to cut its capital-budget allocation process and staffing by a third. This time, the reengineering team got the right people and processes together, solicited employee feedback, and was able to deliver some quick hits. According to John Carl, Executive VP and Chief Financial Officer, the right people were not on the teams originally assigned to reengineer the capital budgeting and planning processes. Capital budgeting and planning *looked* like staff functions, so staff people were assigned to reengineer them. "Success came when we populated the teams...with both line and staff managers," Carl reports. Success, in this case, meant that they were able to complete a capital allocation process in three months, instead of the usual 10, using 250 employees, not 750. And they kept the process tightly integrated with Amoco's overall performance plans and strategies.

THE "JAWS" OF CULTURE

"A corporation's culture can be its greatest strength when it is consistent with its strategies. But a culture that prevents a company from meeting competitive threats, or from adapting to changing economic or social environments, can lead to the company's stagnation and ultimate demise."
—*Business Week*, Oct. 1980

We believe that more reengineering and process improvement efforts fail as a result of cultural issues than any other single reason. If the cultural barriers were well understood and addressed, a much higher percentage of reengineering efforts would achieve their potential.

Just a few of the cultural barriers that cause many reengineering efforts to fail are listed below:

- Hierarchical structure and top-down leadership style
- No established or "felt" need for change
- Internal competition between departments—turf
- Heavy entitlement mind-set and poor empowerment
- Lack of accountability, excessive blaming
- An "observer-critic" culture that kills new ideas
- Communication barriers
- Resistance to changing the status quo
- Reinforcement systems that ignore customer satisfaction
- Non-participative management style—boss-driven command and control
- Lack of trust and respect for individuals
- Top management doesn't really buy-in to the change process

All change initiatives must pass through what we call the "jaws" of culture...most get chewed-up, spit out and forgotten long before they ever accomplish their objectives.

CSC Index has reached a similar conclusion in recently conducting research on 50 clients who had gone through a major reengineering effort. The purpose was to delineate the most frequent and recurring "Stress Points" during the reengineering process. Of the 20 Stress Points identified as classical and reoc-

Cultural Barriers

© 1994 Senn Delaney Leadership Consulting Group, Inc.

curring, the majority seem to be so imbedded in corporate culture that they were given highly descriptive names. These include:

- Smoke & Fire
- Sniping & Rumor Mongering
- Ownership Struggle
- Wet Blankets
- Informed Resistance

These and other names were descriptive of people issues with cultural undertones. While the resistance is indicative of fear, anxiety, and resistance to change, all too often these are seen as the reactions of insecure or "difficult" individuals, instead of being seen as clues of an overall resistant corporate culture. One or two insecure individuals do not kill or stifle a reengineering effort. But those negative individuals, imbedded in a culture that supports their "Smoke Screens" and other diversions, can effectively bring an otherwise well designed reengineering process to a screeching halt.

In the past two decades, many new approaches have emerged to improve business performance. Too often, however, a new theory appears and is hailed as "the answer" only to be later tossed aside as ineffective. We now know that this repeating pattern has less to do with the quality of the ideas than it does with the corporate culture that ground it down.

Trying to apply improvement methods to an unreceptive culture is like trying to apply a band-aid underwater. There's nothing wrong with the band-aid but it won't stick and, therefore, it's completely ineffective. Some organizations benefited greatly from quality circles, MBO, self-managed teams, empowerment, excellence, Theory Z, etc. ...but most tried them, decided they didn't work and moved on to the next quick fix. It wasn't that the theory didn't have value (even when they weren't absolutely perfect); it's that they were applied to an incompatible culture where the new approaches couldn't "take."

One example is IBM. Historically they were at the vanguard of companies that adopted new improvement processes such as quality, empowerment, and customer service. Somehow all these improvement efforts didn't stop IBM's downward momentum. By simply layering these processes onto an existing culture that was rigid, cautious, and fragmented, most of their power to effectively create change was lost. It has taken a revolution at the top of the organization, with the first ever selection of an "outsider" as CEO, to begin to break the old IBM culture and prepare the company for a new, faster moving, more competitive marketplace. Can IBM really make a comeback? How it deals with the entrenched culture of entitlement and hierarchy will provide a significant clue to the future success of IBM.

At the other end of the change spectrum is Ford Motor Company. In the first two years of the 1980s, Ford lost $3 billion and produced cars that were rated in the bottom quartile of quality. However, by 1988, Ford's profits had reached $5.3 billion and its cars consistently ranked in the top 10% of quality. To make this massive transformation, Ford had to change its culture of rigid hierarchy driven by financial considerations to a flexible team-oriented organization concerned with quality and customer service.

The culture of an organization must adapt to new business realities, and what works at one stage in a company's growth may not work at a later stage. Very often, the culture that brought the organization success in its early years may be the very cause of a company's demise. The trick is to recognize this problem and look for ways to shift the culture. All too often the temptation to work harder with old cultural behaviors can lead the organization down a path from which it is difficult to return.

How Culture Impacts Reengineering

While the plans and flow charts that wallpaper the reengineering team room may be impressive and the potential savings and improvements look huge, the reality is that reengineering really takes place in the hearts and minds of employees, not documents and statistics! An old saying we remember from an early college marketing course says it best: "It may be nutritious dog food, the packaging might really sizzle, and the owners may purchase it, but if the dogs don't like it, you're out of luck!"

Between Plans and Reality lay years of habits, customs, unwritten ground rules, parochialism, and vested interests: the corporate culture. Culture can not only stop a reengineering effort dead in its tracks, it can also propel it to great heights. Wisdom is understanding the power of culture and how to get it to work for you instead of against you during reengineering.

Barriers are often hidden in the fabric of the culture and not easy to see without the aid of a comprehensive "Culture Audit." Cultural barriers can quickly show up in terms of dysfunctional behaviors once the reengineering process begins. Key among the early behavior signs of cultural resistance are:

- Reluctance to accept ideas from other organizations and benchmarking comparisons (the "not-invented-here" syndrome)
- Lack of willingness to give up good people to the Reengineering team
- Groups forming under the protection of a politically strong individual who distance themselves from the process
- Senior management having other priorities that prevent sufficient personal involvement and visibility
- Keeping the old process and systems in place in some areas (like finance)
- Work slowdowns, grumbling, and increased labor relations problems
- Lip-service and "Malicious obedience"
- Heavy dependency by members of the Reengineering team to seek the approval from their bosses as opposed to working through the Reengineering Steering Committee

Columbia Gas System: Overcoming Cultural Barriers

When The Columbia Gas System decided to begin a company-wide reengineering process, it asked for help from Arthur Andersen LLP. Early on in the reengineering analysis phase, CEO John Croom was advised that a cultural change would greatly enhance the level of success of the reengineering process that was being contemplated. They felt the traditional utility culture at Columbia was too highly "departmentalized" to support the inter-company coordination required of a successful reengineering effort. While John Croom fully understood that the traditional utility culture was a barrier, he had not fully appreciated the contribution a cultural change could make to the reengineering effort and the need for the change to begin with senior management. The real barrier seemed to be an inordinate amount of corporate controls and analyses being placed on the operating units. The traditional utility bureaucracy was bogging down the change process.

Once John Croom and the senior officers realized the impact of a traditional top-down utility culture on reengineering, they invited Senn-Delaney Leadership to design a culture-shaping initiative to help break down bureaucratic procedures and other cultural barriers and build a sense of teamwork and openness to change that would support the reengineering effort. An off-site senior Executive Retreat for the Columbia Gas senior executives resulted in a new focus on leadership and culture, culminating in a renewed sense of spirit: a statement they call The Spirit of Columbia.

As Senior Vice President, Logan W. Wallingford states:

> *"We were well into our reengineering effort and the consultants from Arthur Andersen who were advising us made a big point that the corporate culture needed to be changed in order for reengineering to succeed.*

> *"Realizing that it would be difficult to successfully continue reengineering with the existing culture, we decided to embark upon a culture change process. We began by taking the senior management team off-site to build the necessary commitment and the appropriate role models at the top.*

"We decided to begin our culture change program with our senior management. We called this first effort our Hershey experience because we met in Hershey, Pennsylvania, and it gave us a chance to rejuvenate our spirits. We rolled it down through the management committees of our various operating committees. Senn-Delaney Leadership trained our own managers as facilitators to take the program on down through the operation.

"Because of the changes going on in our industry, we felt there was a need to really look at our culture and not only revive our spirits but also recapture some of the synergy, cooperation and communication between companies that we had somehow lost. That was our major intent so the title of our culture change program was "The Spirit of Columbia." This process brought together people from across the various divisions of the companies and there is an increased exchange of ideas and understanding and appreciation. Study groups of employees have been formed to generate input into the reengineering process."

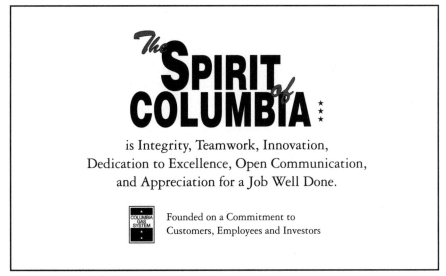

The **SPIRIT** *of* **COLUMBIA** ★★★
is Integrity, Teamwork, Innovation,
Dedication to Excellence, Open Communication,
and Appreciation for a Job Well Done.

Founded on a Commitment to
Customers, Employees and Investors

Successes in the reengineering process at Columbia Gas began to accelerate as the culture began to shift. According to

Mike Casdorph, Senior Vice President for Columbia Gas Transmission Corporation, the System's principal pipeline subsidiary:

> *"We've taken great strides to emphasize the customer and the fact that in our new competitive environment, customers will be making decisions based not only on price, but also on quality and reliability of the service. That's now a primary emphasis throughout Columbia Transmission.*

Ultimately, Casdorph reports, Columbia Transmission "went from five management layers to three between a front-line worker and the top management of the company" as a result of its reengineering efforts.

Columbia Gas was fortunate to discover early that its culture was a stumbling block to its reengineering efforts. Most companies don't find out until they are bogged down and trying to figure out why their reengineering efforts are not working.

SUMMARY

Our own consulting experience with clients undergoing significant process changes suggests that there are a number of cultural elements that must be in place for effective reengineering:

- An understanding of the "unwritten ground rules" in the old culture
- A process to reshape the corporate culture based on healthy shared values
- Strong, inspiring, and committed leadership
- Good communications in all directions ("Overcommunications" is the key)
- Continuity of leadership (don't change horses in mid-stream)
- Direct confrontation of high-level backsliders

Perhaps the biggest factor in the culture which will instantly spell success or failure for reengineering efforts is the degree of openness and the ability of employees at all levels to engage in frank and honest discussions about the business. Without this as a part of the corporate culture, implementation will be decidedly more difficult.

The real performance-enhancing value of reengineering is gained only after fundamental changes in culture, organizational design, management style, leadership, and work practices have been undertaken by a company.

The remaining chapters in this book address the issue of corporate culture during reengineering and how to shift a culture to make it more supportive of performance improvement efforts. Only when the culture is in alignment with the reengineering process can the startling improvements of reengineering be achieved.

Reader Activity

The "Cost of Culture"

A recent study of Fortune 1000 companies by Accountemps estimated that 20% of peoples' time in an organization is wasted on issues related to the corporate culture. Our own observations indicate that time lost on just one cultural barrier: "Victim Games," wastes at least this much time alone! These victim games induce blaming others, justifying poor performance, complaining about what's not working or why things should be different, and are key elements of the cost of culture.

How much is your current corporate culture costing you in terms of lost dollars? The following is a simple and interesting worksheet that can help you get an estimate of the impact of culture on performance.

1. Assemble your senior management team and ask them each to write down an estimate of the % of the work day that is "lost" to such cultural issues as: complaining about other people, talking about management or other departments' actions, blaming others, finding excuses or fault, complaining about lack of direction, etc. Ask them to write down a % (usually it is between 5–25%) representing the time that is wasted and lost.

2. Add up everyone's estimate and get an average:

    _____ Average % of time lost

3. Next determine the total number of employees in your company (or group)

    _____ Number of employees

4. What is the average yearly salary including benefits?

    $ _____

5. Multiply step 3 (number of employees) and step 4 (average salary plus benefits)

    $ _____ Total Yearly Payroll Cost

6. Multiply step 2 (average % of time lost) and step 5 (total yearly payroll cost)

    $ _____ Estimate of lost payroll $$ = "Cost"
    of Culture

What would your income statement look like with those dollars added in to the bottom line? How much easier would the organization be to manage and how much more time would be available to get things done?

3

⁂

CHARTING A NEW COURSE:
REENGINEERING, LEADERSHIP AND CULTURE CHANGE

"First we shape our institutions, and afterwards they shape us."

—Winston Churchill

Lynne Markus, associate professor of Information Science at Claremont Graduate School, concludes, from her research sponsored by the Council of the Society for Information Management, that reengineering is the wrong word and implies a mechanical, programmatic view of the process. Instead, Markus believes that successful reengineering is driven by lots of "Blood, Sweat, and Tears." (*Informationweek,* June 20, 1994)

The failure of many organizational improvement initiatives can generally be traced back to the corporate culture: people resisting change, poor leadership skills, people not knowing how to work together, or people not understanding the new direction. Since reengineering requires a "fundamental rethinking" and perhaps the most far reaching change of any business improvement initiative, it can easily generate the most extensive resistance. Because reengineering pushes all the human boundaries in an organization, it is much more susceptible to failure caused by cultural barriers.

According to Michael Yount, head of the Business Process Improvement team at Transcontinental Gas Pipeline Company, the point to be aware of is that **"you've really failed to fully reengineer until you've shifted the culture as well."**

Before we can create a culture that supports reengineering efforts, it's important to understand how a culture that works perfectly fine under one set of circumstances, can create failure in an environment of reengineering. It helps to take a macro look at an organization as a working relationship between strategy, structure and culture. The following model is one we have used extensively with clients to help them understand how change and culture interact and how corporate culture often acts as a barrier to strategic change.

ALIGNING STRATEGY, STRUCTURE AND CULTURE

Our change management research and client experiences have shown us that unless culture is properly aligned with business strategies, it is difficult, if not impossible, to implement a new strategic thrust to meet increased competition or economic change. In fact, if the new strategies are dramatically different from the old, the culture is likely to conflict with the new direction. The new strategies will be ignored or sabotaged and generally fail. An organization with a firmly embedded culture will find change slow as the culture reinforces and perpetuates the status quo. Thus, the challenge is to shift the culture into alignment with the new business strategy.

In the early growth of an organization, a culture emerges that is influenced by and, in turn, supportive of the organization's strategy and structure (Figure 3.1). One author insightfully describes culture as a group's "shared learning" as it struggles to survive in its environment; it is "the solution to external and internal problems that has worked consistently for a group..." (Schein, Edgar H., *How Culture Forms, Develops and Changes*. Jossey-Bass, Inc., 1985, page 19). Thus, culture develops over time,

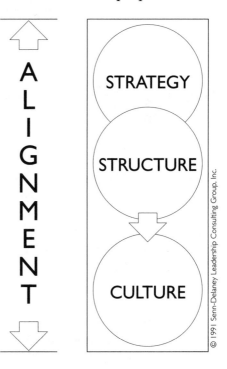

Figure 3.1

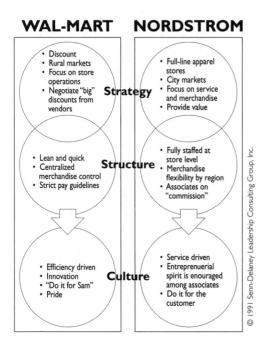

WAL-MART   NORDSTROM

Strategy
- Discount
- Rural markets
- Focus on store operations
- Negotiate "big" discounts from vendors

- Full-line apparel stores
- City markets
- Focus on service and merchandise
- Provide value

Structure
- Lean and quick
- Centralized merchandise control
- Strict pay guidelines

- Fully staffed at store level
- Merchandise flexibility by region
- Associates on "commission"

Culture
- Efficiency driven
- Innovation
- "Do it for Sam"
- Pride

- Service driven
- Entreprenuerial spirit is enouraged among associates
- Do it for the customer

© 1991 Senn-Delaney Leadership Consulting Group, Inc.

Figure 3.2

evolving in response to the demands of the internal and external environment. While early cultures are relatively "soft" and formative, later they harden, taking on an existence of their own.

Within the US retail industry, it is easy to see this model in action. Wal-Mart pursues a mass-merchandising discount strategy, while Nordstrom, also financially successful, depends on a strategy of providing a full-line of soft goods with a significant focus on extraordinary customer service. Both Wal-Mart and Nordstrom are large, nation-wide organizations that have been able to evolve strong cultures that are in alignment with their respective strategies and structures (Figure 3.2).

Indeed, many industry observers agree that it is the strength of the Wal-Mart and Nordstrom cultures (which are very different yet equally strong) that make both organizations able to implement plans better than their competitors. While the competition may pursue similar strategies, they do so with less aligned or cohesive corporate cultures and achieve significantly less impressive results. Wal-Mart and Nordstrom developed completely different strategies, structures and cultures, yet each organization is a highly aligned and productive organization with a vital competitive advantage.

When organizations face changes in their business environments, survival and prosperity often depend on their ability to quickly change directions. Generally this involves a shift in strategy followed by changes in organizational structure (Figure 3.3).

As new strategies are developed and new structures put into place, many employees continue to think and perform in ways that were developed within the old culture. These methods of working and managing are often "at odds" with the new strategy and organizational structure. While the corporate goals have shifted, the old ways of doing business are still in place and may now be in conflict with the new directions.

There are several signs that a corporate culture has gotten out of alignment with the organization's strategy and structure:

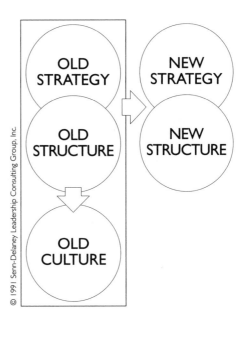

© 1991 Senn-Delaney Leadership Consulting Group, Inc.

Figure 3.3

- frequent reorganizations, but the same old problems persist;
- unwillingness to take risks, or make long-term commitments;
- resistance to new ways of doing things;
- lack of accountability...spending time blaming or finding fault;
- power plays and poor teamwork, causing costly project delay or errors;
- mistrust between management and employees; and
- lack of clear vision or direction; people are confused about where they're going.

In an organization that is "out of alignment," more and more effort is required to "make things work" as the organization struggles to meet the challenges of today with the "atti-

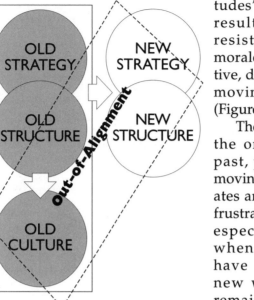

Figure 3.4

tudes" of yesterday. The result is often tension, resistance and lowered morale instead of an effective, dynamic organization moving toward its goals (Figure 3.4).

The old culture anchors the organization in the past, preventing it from moving forward. This creates an increasing level of frustration which becomes especially pronounced when some employees have "bought into" the new way, while others remain mired in the old. One manager described this stage of change as pushing a rope: "there's a great deal of effort expended, but it doesn't seem to get you anywhere."

The challenge of leadership is to shift the culture into alignment with the new strategy and structure. We like to think in terms of shifting a culture as opposed to replacing it, as key cultural characteristics usually exist that should be retained and nurtured, while new characteristics will need to be added to make the culture more compatible with the new strategic thrust (Figure 3.5).

A "Universal" Example

The Bell Telephone System is a classic example of the effect of a changing industry on the alignment of strategy, structure and culture. For more than half a century, "universal service, end-to-end" was the Bell corporate vision and they were very good at it. Every component in the organization–financial policies, technology, pricing philosophy, product and market strategies and organizational design–evolved to support this pervasive mission.

Overall, the Bell System's strategies were driven by regulatory and technological considerations. Financial policies were geared toward dividends, with a heavy debt structure and extensive external financing. Bell Laboratories, insulated in the regulated environment, was able to focus on basic research and technological opportunity, without worrying about consumer preferences. Customer pricing, which was subsidized by the overall rate base, was based on the premise that everyone should be able to afford phone ser-

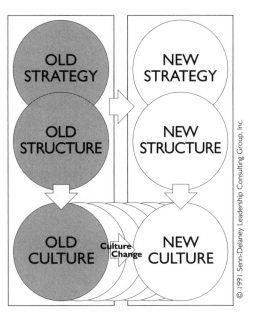

Figure 3.5

vice. Marketing and product strategies focused on mass markets and standardized products. The corporate structure was large, centralized, and organized by function.

The Bell corporate culture included a "regulatory mind-set" that favored adherence to policies and procedures, rigorous analysis of new projects and changes, and an elaborate approval process. The reward system fostered lifetime careers, with a slow, steady progression and a strong focus on hierarchy. Other characteristics of the culture included dedication to customer service, group accountability, standardized procedures and formal communication. The culture was ideally aligned with the organization's structure and strategy of universal service.

W. Brooke Tunstall, an AT&T vice president who was closely involved in the divestiture planning leading up to the 1984 breakup of AT&T, provides an inside view of the cultural dynamics at AT&T in his book *"Disconnecting Parties"*:

"All these (cultural) attributes evolved to directly support one superordinate goal, universal service. In fact, everything related to the culture was affected by this goal; the kind of people we hired, their shared value systems, the infrastructure of processes to run the business. All were committed to the unchanging objective of providing high-quality service at affordable prices to everyone in the United States. Rarely, in fact, had corporate mission and corporate culture been so ideally matched."

In the years preceding the January 1984 divestiture, the telecommunications industry experienced a dramatic change, as it began the shift from a monopolistic, regulated environment to a competitive, deregulated one. After divestiture, AT&T and the new "Baby Bells" responded with numerous changes in strategy and structure.

New strategic directions were driven by market opportunities and financial needs. Financial strategies were geared to meet earnings-per-share growth objectives, with a much lower debt structure. Research and design efforts would shift toward the application of technology to meet customer requirements. Markets would be segmented, with customized offerings. Finally, the organization would be restructured into smaller, more decentralized business units to better support the markets and the customer-driven strategies.

It's easy to imagine the tension as employees struggled (some even still) to meet the demands of the new strategies, with a culture which had previously been developed for the regulated business environment. Following the 1984 breakup, a corporate survey at AT&T asked 6,000 employees to share their thoughts and feelings surrounding various aspects of the divestiture and the new organizations. The findings revealed somewhat of an identity crisis for the AT&T employees with the following summarizing the general feelings:

"I knew the old Bell system, its mission, its operation, its people, its culture. And I knew my niche in it. In that knowledge, I had identity and confidence about my company and myself. Now I work for a new company, one fourth its former size, with only a partial history and no track record. With the loss of our

mission, Universal Service, and the fragmentation of the very business of providing telephone service, I find myself asking, 'Who are we? Who am I?'"

The 1984 divestiture created organizational chaos. Suddenly employees and organizations were in a world of competition, where the ability to deliver the products and services customers preferred at a price they were willing to pay was critical to survival. While the leaders of these "new" organizations quickly recognized the need to change strategies and organizational structures, they soon found themselves with companies out of alignment. Over the past 10 years, culture change has been a key ingredient in the success of the Baby Bells.

New Strategies and Old Cultures: A Design To Fail

In the business world prior to 1980, a relatively stable business environment supported cultures that were highly structured, with carefully developed standards and procedures, clearly defined policies, multilayered organization charts, strong chain-of-command, deliberate approval processes, and a compensation system that rewarded "playing by the rules." Since the game wasn't changing much, neither should the rules!

Today's current environment of increased global competition, rapid technological advances, worldwide economic fluctuations and changing social norms and values has upset all the old rules and thrown out all the standard success formulas. These extraordinary changes are forcing today's business leaders to shift not only strategy and structure, but culture as well.

Jack Welch, Chairman and CEO of General Electric states that fundamental change is a fact of life that's here to stay.

"Organizations are changing by necessity. Globalization is simply a fact of life. We have slower growth in the developed worlds. This puts more pressure on all of us since we are all after a piece of the pie. Therefore, value is all there is to provide. For example, in the computer business, if you miss a cycle you lose your company. So if you're going to provide

the most value, if you're going to have the lowest cost and the highest quality product available, you've got to engage every mind that you hire. To have some minds idling in a stalled mode is unacceptable."

As companies scramble to change their strategy and structure, they're finding themselves anchored by a culture that's stuck in the old ways. Trying to implement new strategies and structures with an out-of-alignment culture creates a chaotic environment that spreads confusion, disrupts morale and can actually lower productivity.

This reaction is especially likely in an organization that decides to embark on reengineering because, by definition, reengineering requires fundamental change and rethinking of cross-functional processes. Therefore, it is important for an organization to address the issue of corporate culture early in the reengineering process and to link the two change efforts together.

4

LINKING REENGINEERING AND CULTURE CHANGE

Reengineering and culture change are natural partners in the performance improvement process.

Reengineering efforts are most successful in cultures that support change. When this is not the case, a culture-shaping process should precede or at a minimum be concurrent with reengineering. A good rule for change is: "Don't plant seeds on barren ground!" Bell Atlantic preceded its reengineering with The Bell Atlantic Way process to create a new, high-performance culture. When Columbia Gas was told that to be successful, reengineering would require a cultural change, it implemented a concurrent teambuilding and culture change process it calls "The Spirit of Columbia."

Fred Musone, President of Federal Mogul led the reengineering effort that cut sample development time from 20 weeks to 18 days. He states,

"We had to get radically better...it was an easy decision because our future was at risk. When we got started, I went down to the factory and stood on a bunch of pallets and told people what I saw about the company and its past and future. I shared my thoughts and told them that if we were going to have a future, we were going to have to get a whole lot better.

"Then, before we started to change anything, we put every single person in the company through a session led by the local leadership. That session did not have one single thing to do with answering the question 'How to?' It was a session totally dedicated to why we should change. Once everyone knows 'why' and believes it, the 'how to' is easy. We do not

*have a problem with the lack of intelligence or strength...it's
the lack of will that creates failures. Will comes from understanding why we do things."*

In its broadest contexts, the processes of reengineering and
culture change are naturally linked in a number of ways:

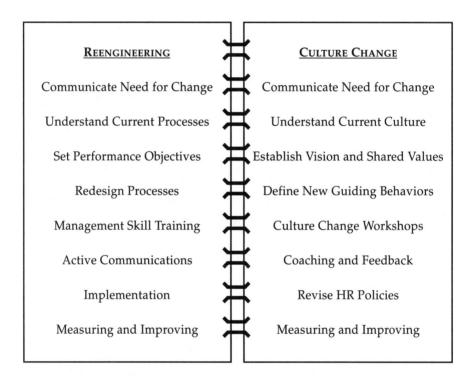

REENGINEERING	CULTURE CHANGE
Communicate Need for Change	Communicate Need for Change
Understand Current Processes	Understand Current Culture
Set Performance Objectives	Establish Vision and Shared Values
Redesign Processes	Define New Guiding Behaviors
Management Skill Training	Culture Change Workshops
Active Communications	Coaching and Feedback
Implementation	Revise HR Policies
Measuring and Improving	Measuring and Improving

The primary focus of this book is **How to Create a Culture
that Supports Change.** This is best seen in the context of a
change like reengineering. To show how culture change and
reengineering are linked, we will use a successful reengineering process model and match it with a culture change process
pioneered by our staff at Senn-Delaney Leadership.

A MODEL FOR CULTURE CHANGE

"Necessity is the Mother of Invention"

—Anonymous

Our journey to better understand the power of corporate culture and to create an effective culture-shift process began about 25 years ago. The original Senn-Delaney organization was a performance improvement consulting firm. In trying to improve productivity we were struck by the fact that it was hard to implement change in some companies, yet so easy in others. We began to note that companies seemed to have "personalities," like people, each with some positive traits, but also with some personality defects.

While some clients tended to operate like high-performance teams, all too many seemed like dysfunctional families. One consulting engagement illustrated this dramatically. We were retained to improve productivity and reduce the processing time in a large mid-West distribution center of a major retail company. Their own studies showed that costs were 20%–25% too high and inventory turnaround time too slow. They had invested several million dollars in new warehousing mechanization, and had even fired two facility mangers who "weren't getting the job done." Still they were far short of their performance objectives and the stores were screaming for merchandise sooner. They asked Senn-Delaney to analyze the layout, methods and systems to see what barriers to efficiency we could find. At first we were puzzled because we couldn't find anything really wrong with the systems or their procedures.

However, we did notice something else. Everyone at the facility we spoke with agreed that performance was terrible, and they were all convinced it was someone else's fault! The checkers blamed the markers, the markers blamed the ticket makers, the ticket makers blamed the vendors, the supervisors blamed the labor pool they had to draw from, and one person on the shipping dock was even convinced it was the company's fault because they didn't provide warm enough jackets during the winter! This facility had an almost terminal case of "lack of accountability" and we could almost see the invisible walls that separated each department's "turf."

We decided to focus more of our attention on creating team behaviors and less on traditional system redesign efforts. We developed an innovative off-site retreat for the facility managers and supervisors and focused on the concepts of accountability (instead of blaming), openness to change (instead of resistance and fear), and cross-departmental teamwork (instead of turf battles). Back at the Distribution Center we focused management on coaching these new behaviors to an equal extent with their already good focus on the numbers.

Within 90 days productivity was up 30% and turnaround time cut by over a third. Team spirit was also up and subsequent employee surveys showed marked improvement in employee satisfaction. We knew we were on to something but didn't fully understand it yet.

Experiences like the above and others led to research work as a part of a doctoral program at the University of Southern California for Larry Senn. That culminated in a dissertation (Organizational Character as a Tool in the Analysis of Business Organizations, USC, 1970) based on the first systematic field studies done in America on the phenomenon we now call corporate culture.

The Culture Change model presented here is the result of our consulting work with Fortune 1000 companies over the past 16 years and has proven to be effective in such diverse industries as Financial Services, Health Care, Nuclear Power, Telecommunications, Manufacturing, Distribution, Retailing, and other industries.

There are no magic formulas for organizational change, no quick fixes. However, through our consulting experience we've developed an integrated process for shifting culture, which when led by senior management, has proven to be highly effective. An overview of the Senn-Delaney Leadership Culture Change Model is described below and then integrated with a Reengineering Model. Each phase of the culture change process is then explored in detail during subsequent chapters.

Senn-Delaney Leadership Process for Culture Change

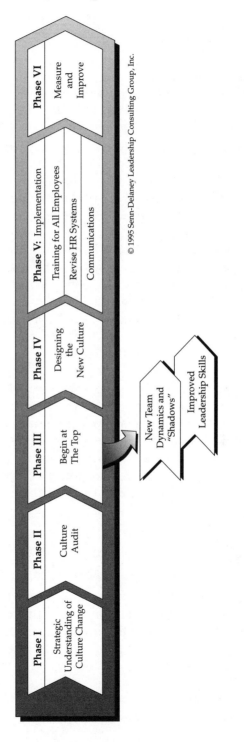

Phase I	Phase II	Phase III	Phase IV	Phase V: Implementation	Phase VI
Strategic Understanding of Culture Change	Culture Audit	Begin at The Top	Designing the New Culture	Training for All Employees / Revise HR Systems / Communications	Measure and Improve

New Team Dynamics and "Shadows"

Improved Leadership Skills

> *Phase I:*
> *Strategic Understanding of Culture Change*

The Strategic Understanding of Culture Change is the important first step that helps an organization see the impact of culture on organizational performance. It is useful here to educate management on what culture is, where it comes from, how it impacts performance, and the overall process for culture change. It is also important at this initial stage to begin a general discussion about what changes are happening in their industry and why the culture needs to change.

Since change is a function of perceived need, Phase I is also a time to educate the entire Senior Management Team on the overall principles of culture change and their role in reshaping it. Even though most managers expend a significant amount of their time and energy dealing with cultural barriers, nowhere in their careers have they been taught the skills of shaping culture.

It is important at this critical educational phase to examine examples of other companies who have gone through successful culture change. It is often useful to:

- Invite the CEO or other senior executives from a few of these companies to talk to the senior management team.
- Have open and frank discussions about the need for "personal" change as well as organizational change
- Do some outside reading
- Learn more about what culture is; how cultures are built; what the difference is between a strong and a weak culture

> *Phase II:*
> *The Culture Audit and Gap Analysis*

In reengineering, benchmarking and baseline measurement is important to conduct early on in the process. These activities define the magnitude of the opportunity and establish a starting point for measuring progress. Parallels exist in cultural reengineering as well:

- What is the level of readiness for change?
- How deep are issues of mistrust?

- How aligned is the senior team?
- What is the level of teamwork between departments?
- What are the key cultural barriers to change?
- What cultural and organizational changes are needed to support reengineering?

These and other questions need to be fully answered and understood before culture change can begin.

The underlying cultural barriers to reengineering are not always obvious and it is often difficult for those inside the organization to clearly see their own culture. That is why it is useful to take advantage of an "outsider's view" in analyzing and shaping corporate culture.

The process of taking a culture audit (a "snapshot" of the current culture) is not quite as straightforward as in the more technical Benchmarking study. Since culture is a holistic concept, much like an ecosystem, the interrelationships between cultural behaviors are as meaningful as the individual behaviors themselves. The broader question to be answered is "What's really going on here? What's the story?" and "What are the implications for reengineering?"

The "story" can best be visualized and described through a culture audit, which is an active process of one-on-one interviews, evaluations of current planning documents, assessment of existing HR policies, review of corporate history, and an understanding of the industry and its driving forces. Measurement tools such as our own Corporate Culture Profile℠ and Guiding Behaviors Inventory℠ are also helpful in establishing a profile of the current culture, and its strengths and weaknesses.

Phase III:
Begin at the Top

This is the most critical phase and builds on the premise that organizations are "shadows of their leaders." For a culture-shift to truly take root, the top management team must become role models of the new cultural values and guiding behaviors.

This stage requires introspection and self-assessment on the part of senior management. The CEO and each member of the senior management team must ask themselves the following:

- What role model do I present to the organization?
- What kind of shadow do I cast?
- Am I, as a member of the senior management team, in alignment with our mission and values?

Communication and teamwork barriers must first be overcome at the top. A clear vision of the new culture must be collectively developed and thoroughly understood at the senior-most level before it can be actively implemented and translated into the day-to-day policy and behavior changes necessary to shift a culture.

All too often organizations hire training companies to implement "Employee Development Programs," "Change-Management Skills" or "Quality Improvement" programs for middle managers, expecting that these programs will bring about the desired changes. And all too often, nothing significant happens because it was not supported and role-modeled from the top.

To insure cultural transformation there must be a shift in the behavior of the senior management team. It is absolutely critical to establish leadership alignment and role models at the top. The senior management team needs to interact and communicate in ways that model the new desired culture. It is during this phase that senior management commits to becoming true champions of the new culture and shift their own behavior first, before they ask others to adopt the new culture.

The central activity of Phase III is a well-designed, off-site retreat where members of the senior team better understand the strengths and weaknesses of the corporate culture, as well as the senior team itself, and together explore their roles as leaders of a new, high-performance culture.

As the senior team begins to exhibit new levels of teamwork, openness, communications, and overall leadership they begin to truly champion the culture change process.

Phase IV:
Designing the New Culture

Deciding on the "New" Culture helps the organization identify a new set of Shared Values and Guiding Behaviors that will allow the company to be even more successful in a changing business environment. In addition, it is important to develop a clear vision for the organization that will easily communicate to all employees "who we are," "where we are going," and "what is important."

This phase involves a careful examination of the organization's strategy and structure by the senior management team; it is their responsibility to develop a new cultural model and to define those values and behaviors that are consistent with the overall business strategy. This will include identifying those current values and behaviors that should be maintained, those which should be discouraged, and those which need to be developed.

This new cultural model must be consistent with the overall strategic and business plans, while addressing the competitive pressures from the business environment. It should present clear benefits for the company as a whole, for individual employees and for stockholders. The most effective cultural ingredients will be realistic, easily communicated to all levels of the organization, and capable of implementation through training and changes in various systems and structures.

The bottom line question is: Will these values and behaviors allow the reengineering process to go forward successfully? Will they help improve our competitive advantage?

Phase V:
Implementation

Implementation focuses on the activities of Training, Revising HR Systems, and Communications, each of which is crucial to the implementation of the new culture. Culture change workshops similar to the session developed for the senior team can be developed for all employees so they can have a meaningful experience of the new culture. In these special, highly interactive workshops, new behaviors and expectations are not only discussed, but "lived."

It is also important to review and revise the HR systems
and policies so that they are aligned with the new vision and
values. Communication also plays a critical part in the overall
shifting of the culture, and multiple formats for communicating to employees, customers, shareholders, the Board of Direc-
tors, vendors and suppliers, and even the families of
employees need to be developed and implemented.

Phase VI:
Measurement and Ongoing Improvement

Measurement and Improvement is ongoing and provides for
the development of feedback mechanisms to measure the
progress of the culture change. Cultural alignment is a continuous process, not a series of static events, as changing business
conditions will continue to impact the organization. Experience
has shown that the process of shaping a new culture throughout a firm takes approximately two to three years. And that's
with an active culture change program!

Follow-up seminars are useful in reinforcing the new ways
of thinking and working, and should be implemented on an
ongoing basis. Regular communications should be sent to all
employees to share the progress and reinforce the momentum
of the culture-shift.

Several methods can be used to assist in the evaluation and
feedback process. A tracking system can measure where the
"cultural gaps" exist (those disparities between where an organization is and where it wants to be). Specially designed feedback instruments should be implemented on a regular basis.
One of the best tools for measuring the shift in culture is a 360°
Feedback Profile. This powerful tool is developed around the
values and behaviors necessary for the new culture and provides valuable insight into the level of acceptance of the new
culture. Feedback gives management a basis for further development and implementation of the desired culture change.
(See Chapter 10 for more information about the 360° as a feedback and measurement tool.)

A BUSINESS PROCESS REENGINEERING MODEL

Over the years we have worked on parallel culture change processes with half a dozen different reengineering firms. Each has its own model. In the right culture, all can be successful.

The model for Business Process Reengineering described in this chapter is the one currently in use by the Business Consulting Practice of Arthur Andersen LLP. The original model was developed in the mid-1980s and has evolved over the past ten years from experience on hundreds of engagements around the world.

The underlying principles include:

- Integrated high performing client/consultant teams.
- Focus on high value opportunities derived from fact based analysis.
- Development and implementation of solutions aligned with customer needs.
- Increased capacity for organizational learning and change.
- Intensive reexamination of the way a company does business in order to produce dramatic improvements in performance through an alignment of process, people, technology, measurement and organization structure in support of shared vision and values.

This model on the following page is a road map for conducting a reengineering project. While the model serves as a useful road map, it is not a rigid methodology. Any successful approach must be tailored to meet the requirements and culture of the particular company.

This model is useful in communicating to people where they are during the reengineering process and what lies ahead. The structure of the model provides comfort in uncertain times as each phase builds a solid foundation for the next, and because it includes a mechanism for involvement and buy-in at all levels of the organization.

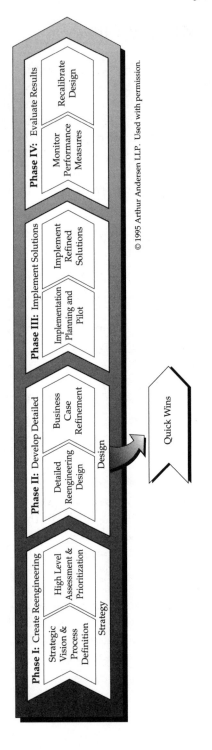

Arthur Andersen Reengineering Model

Phase I: Create Reengineering

| Strategic Vision & Process Definition | High Level Assessment & Prioritization |

Strategy

Phase II: Develop Detailed

| Detailed Reengineering Design | Business Case Refinement |

Design

Phase III: Implement Solutions

| Implementation Planning and Pilot | Implement Refined Solutions |

Phase IV: Evaluate Results

| Monitor Performance Measures | Recalibrate Design |

Quick Wins

Phase I:
Create Reengineering Strategy

The overarching objective of this phase is to filter the opportunities for reengineering and develop hypotheses to achieve the "quantum" leap in performance attributes of quality, cycle time, growth and/or profitability.

Key activities to consider include:

- Assessing customer needs and values
- Performing a benchmarking study
- Analyzing current processes
- Determining "Best Practices"
- Creating initial visions of the future business and processes

During this phase, it is important to create a high performing team balanced between company personnel and consultants. In addition, a comprehensive communication strategy should be designed and implemented. The business purpose justifying a project of this nature must be clearly and vividly articulated.

Phase II:
Develop Detailed Design

The primary result of this phase is the creation of a "blueprint" that guides the implementation of the reengineered environment.

Key activities to be considered include:

- Redesigning business processes adhering to the initial visions developed in Phase I
- Assessing implications and creating solutions associated with other elements of the reengineered environment (e.g., people, technology, business controls, organization structure and performance measures)
- Refining the business case for the change effort including cost/benefit analysis for implementing the redesigned processes

- Implementing "quick-wins" (i.e., opportunities for change that can be readily implemented and provide immediate benefits)

During this phase, it is important to bring fresh, creative insights to the project team. This enables the creation of more "radical" solutions that achieve the reengineering goals. Recognize that there may have to be a balance between these "radical" ideas and a company's ability (both financial and capacity for change) to implement the solutions.

Phase III: Implement Solutions

The objectives of this phase are to successfully implement the reengineered system and design a comprehensive measurement framework for monitoring results.

The key activities of this phase include:

- Testing the reengineered solutions through a pilot implementation
- Measuring the pilot results
- Refining the solutions and preparing detailed implementation plans
- Implementing the refined processes
- Operating the reengineered system

In order to achieve lasting change, the organization must support the pilot through extensive communications, personnel training and monitoring. Management should be flexible in refining the implementation plans based on the pilot results. Also, the creation of new performance measures is important to guide and support the new behaviors required in the reengineered environment.

Phase IV:
Evaluate Results

The results of Phase IV ensure that the expected benefits from reengineering are realized in accordance with the overall vision.

Key activities to consider include the formalization of a continuous improvement program, monitoring of the key performance measures and process results and revising elements of the reengineered environment based on performance analysis.

It is during this phase that cultural shift must be enacted so that employees are empowered to suggest and act upon process deficiencies. In fact, employees should be held accountable for the achievement of specific performance measures.

LINKING REENGINEERING AND CULTURE CHANGE

By integrating these two process models, reengineering and culture change, and understanding both the technical and human side of performance improvement, organizations can create a more complete process for ensuring reengineering success.

As this integrated model shows, the elements of the culture change process blend in at various points to support and reinforce the overall reengineering process. With attention to both the technical and cultural elements involved in performance improvement, we believe that nearly every organization can reap the enormous benefits of reengineering!

While we have used one well-documented reengineering model in this book, the principles of culture change will enhance the results of any reengineering effort or change initiative, including shifts in strategy, restructuring or Total Quality processes.

The following chapters will guide you through each of the phases of culture change and provide specific ideas and activities to help you effectively create a corporate culture which will support your reengineering efforts.

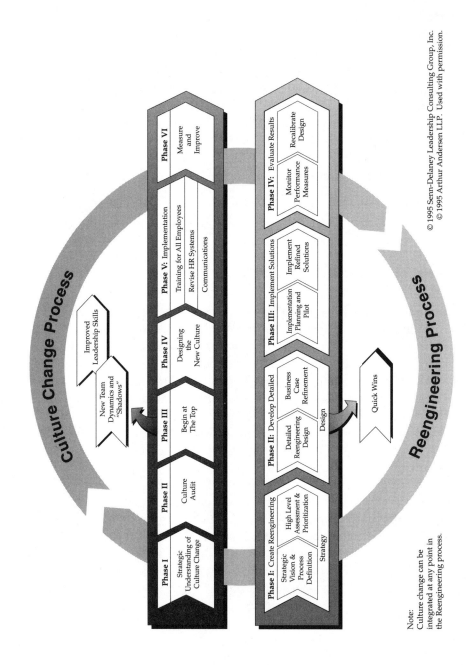

© 1995 Senn-Delaney Leadership Consulting Group, Inc.
© 1995 Arthur Andersen LLP. Used with permission.

Note:
Culture change can be
integrated at any point in
the Reengineering process.

5

PHASE I: STRATEGIC UNDERSTANDING OF CULTURE CHANGE

Hewlett Packard posts record profits—IBM continues layoffs
K-Mart is sluggish—Wal-Mart's growth continues
Federal Express soars—US Postal Service struggles
Ford Motor Co. produces America's best-selling car and higher
profits than GM, the world's largest auto manufacturer

While a set of engineering drawings and specifications can adequately depict the performance of a system or piece of equipment, rarely does the performance of a company live up to the potential depicted in its organizational charts, strategic plans or mission statements. The difference in performance from plan to reality is often significant, and has been the speculation of countless articles and books on motivation, leadership, management skills, and other elements of the "soft side" of business.

But, are these elements really "soft?" While a business plan may look concrete with all of its facts and spreadsheets, it's actually an abstraction. It is an idea for the future and has no real existence in the organization or reality in the marketplace. The corporate culture, however, is a living, breathing dynamic force that has a life of its own, operating independently of all plans and projections yet determining the success or failure of those plans.

The notion that the performance of an organization is dependent upon a set of "organizational behaviors" that are often subjective and intangible is not new. These intangibles, which are far harder to measure than number of shipments or return on equity, are often the key factors in one organization's success compared with another. The difference between success and failure in the business world can often be attributed to a limited set of organizational characteristics that combine to produce the corporate culture.

In a study of more than 200 companies reported in their important book, *Corporate Culture and Performance,* John P. Kotter and James L. Heskett describe how shared values and unwritten rules can profoundly enhance economic success, or conversely, lead to failure to adapt to changing markets and environments.

THE ECONOMICS AND SOCIAL COSTS OF LOW-PERFORMANCE CULTURES (TWELVE-FIRM AVERAGE FOR 1977–1988)	With Performance-Enhancing Cultures (%)	Without Performance-Enhancing Cultures (%)
Revenue Growth	682	166
Employment Growth	282	36
Stock Price Growth	901	74
Tax Base (Net Income) Growth	756	1

Source: *Corporate Culture and Performance,* John P. Kotter and James L. Heskett. Used with permission.

According to Kotter and Heskett,

"Strategy is simply a logic for how to achieve movement in some direction. The beliefs and practices called for in a strategy may be compatible with a firm's culture or they may not. When they are not, a company usually finds it difficult to implement the strategies successfully."

If culture supports the strategy of the organization and if agreement exists among members of the company about the importance of specific, high-performance values, the culture is said to be strong. In a company with a strong culture, you can feel the human energy that flows from aligned committed employees. If little agreement exists, the culture is weak. In a company with a weak culture, the available energy is fragmented and often dissipated through conflicting agendas, blaming, and unclear communications.

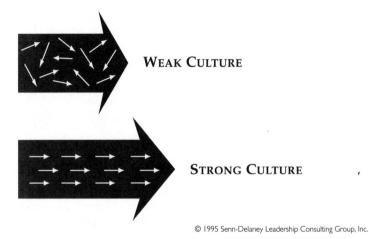

To the leaders of a company, corporate culture represents a powerful force that, with the proper attention and leadership tools, can be focused and managed for the good of the company and its employees. In their book, *Corporate Cultures*, Terrence E. Deal and Allen A. Kennedy emphasize that effective corporate culture helps organizations and people be more productive:

> *"A strong culture is a system of informal rules that spells out how people are to behave most of the time. By knowing what exactly is expected of them, employees will waste little time in deciding how to act in a given situation. In a weak culture, on the other hand, employees waste a good deal of time just trying to figure out what they should do and how they should do it. The impact of a strong culture on productivity is amazing. In the extreme, we estimate that a company can gain as much as one to two hours of productive work per employee per day!"*

In the broadest sense, corporate culture refers to the personality of the organization, the shared beliefs and the written (and unwritten) policies and procedures which determine the ways in which the organization and its people behave and solve business problems. Culture provides the meaning, direction, and clarity (the human glue) that mobilizes the collective energy of a corporation toward goals and accomplishments.

Corporate culture is a composite of the following:

- Shared Values–*What we think is important*
- Beliefs–*How we think things should be done*
- Behaviors–*The way we do things around here*
- Heroes–*The people who personify our corporate culture*
- Systems–*Our written and unwritten policies and procedures*

More simply put, it's "the way we do things around here."

In order to use corporate culture as a tool in Reengineering or any other change, it is important to first understand how a culture is formed and the major ingredients in the development of corporate culture.

THE ORIGIN OF A CORPORATE CULTURE

An individual's personality is the result of genetic inheritance, environmental influences, and current thought processes. Similarly, a corporation's culture is determined by everything that touches it: the industry it's in, the people who work there, its leaders, previous history, customers, suppliers, stockholders, regulatory agencies, community, etc.

Corporate culture is created through the interaction of the critical Key Determinants of Culture:

- Corporate History
- Leadership Style
- Industry and Environment
- Regional Differences
- Employee Base
- Key Organizational Tasks

The following model shows these Key Determinants of Culture and how they interact to form the corporate culture.

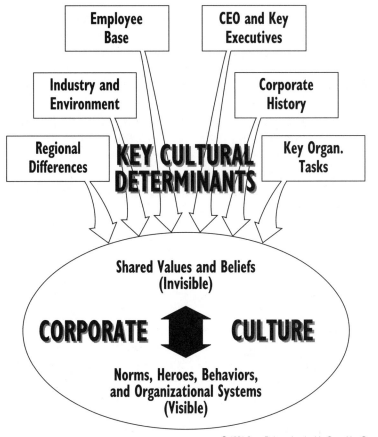

© 1991 Senn-Delaney Leadership Consulting Group, Inc.

Every organization develops its own cultural distinctions based on these key influencing factors:

Corporate History—Nordstrom began as a shoe store. That has greatly influenced its culture. In a well-run, service-oriented shoe store, customers get a lot of special attention. The salesperson measures the customer's feet, goes and gets various styles and sizes of shoes and puts them on the customer's feet. Since most shoe stores operate on commission, a sales consciousness also exists.

From that base, Nordstrom began to add apparel to become a department store but the shoe store traditions carried forward. Is it any wonder that people marvel at how a Nordstrom salesperson will run around the store to find items to complete an outfit?

Apple Computer was begun by two young entrepreneurs whose total focus was to create a personal computer that was easy to operate and user-friendly. In contrast, IBM, a data tabulating company focused on large mainframes, sold to more sophisticated information officers. IBM had to rely upon another young maverick, Bill Gates, to create a PC operating system. Even today Apple's Macintosh operating system is more user-friendly than a DOS-based operating system.

Leadership Style—The most consistent finding from all research done on corporate culture is the following:

Organizations become shadows of their leaders

In every organization there are the shadows cast by current leaders and the ghosts of former leaders. In examining a culture, it is usually easy to determine the impact of current leaders as well as previous leaders. Have the leaders been visionary, restrictive, participative, behind the times, open, secretive, entrepreneurial, status quo, innovative, family-oriented, conservative, etc.?

Ross Perot, founder of EDS, left IBM because it was too slow moving and bureaucratic. He was forceful with a military mind-set, very hard working, goal-oriented, and principled. Many years later that hard working, aggressive quality can still be seen at EDS.

Hewlett Packard had a team-based culture decades before it was the thing to do. That was simply an outgrowth of William Hewlett's and David Packard's philosophy of having smaller team-based units no matter how much the firm grew.

Industry Characteristics—The characteristics of an industry can create dramatically different cultures; such as a defense contractor compared to an advertising agency. In its dealings with the federal government, defense contractors have to adhere to stringent sets of specifications, rules and regulations. This environment tends to attract analytical, thorough and deliberate people who can thrive in an intensely structured milieu. These people hire other people who can handle regulations and insure conformity to standards; they do business with suppliers who fallow regulations and procedures. Gradually the corporate personality grows more distinct and people who do not "fit the mold" opt out or are forced out.

An advertising agency exists in a totally different environment. They require fast-paced people with a high sense of urgency and the ability to make quick decisions based on both consumer data and emotional appeal. They make heroes of people with creative flair and a sense of style and abhor bureaucracies and regulations.

Employee Base—The demographics of the work force play a key role. Some examples are: young, fast-food part-timers; well-educated information workers; skilled production workers; and volunteers. Are employees technically-oriented, creative, risk-averse people, skilled, unskilled, female or male? Retail cultures differ from nuclear utilities in part, because one has a significant percentage of technical people with engineering or science degrees and the other has very few.

Region—Is the firm global or local? Is it headquartered in the Silicon Valley, inner city, rural agricultural area, Pacific Rim, sun belt, Bible belt, university area or midwestern suburbs? Wal-Mart has that folksy feeling in part because it's from Bentonville, Arkansas and not New York City.

Key Tasks—What is the primary product or service? Is it software programming, engineering, retail sales, logging, airport transportation, machinery operation, education, manufacturing? Key tasks reflect the kind of employee base, the nature of industry, leadership style and other determinants of culture.

Imagine the corporate cultures that might result from these two scenarios:

	COMPANY #1	COMPANY #2
Industry ▶	High technology	Retail
Leadership ▶	Entrepreneurial	Finance background
Employee Base ▶	Young, well-educated, salaried professionals	Mostly hourly employees
Key Tasks ▶	Programming	Merchandising
Region ▶	Mountain recreation area	Suburbs
History ▶	Start-up	75 years in business, named after founder

In order to understand your own culture, just give some thought to how it is influenced by the founders, industry, current leaders, employee base and key tasks.

VALUES AND BELIEFS: THE INNER FABRIC OF CULTURE

Key Cultural Determinants interact in various ways to create the inner fabric of corporate culture: the Shared Values and Beliefs. Values are the important philosophical underpinnings of the organization that spell out "what is important" within the company. Values often include Integrity, Concern for Employees, A High Service Ethic, but may also include such business practicalities as loyalty, respect for "position," etc.

Beliefs refer to "the way we are supposed to be around here" and include both empowering and limiting beliefs as:

- we should all work as a team
- keep your head down and don't make waves
- people should follow rules
- follow the chain of command
- have an open door policy
- managers are paid to make decisions
- hourly employees can't be trusted with financial data
- fair pay for a fair day's work
- people need to be motivated
- it is not safe to admit a mistake

When Values and Beliefs are shared by a group of people who work together to accomplish an overall objective, they exert a tremendous power over the attitudes and behaviors of all employees. They become a powerful set of "unwritten" ground rules that guide daily decisions and actions. These shared values and beliefs can be so strong that individuals coming into an organization with a different set of values and beliefs may find it difficult to fit in. Sometimes the person faces a choice of adapting to the rules of the game or leaving the company.

The values that members of an organization share create a template for corporate and individual behavior. Some companies see their corporate values as a source of competitive advantage, allowing the organization and its members to react quickly and decisively to business events and competitive pressures.

James Burke, former chairman of Johnson & Johnson believes that the Johnson & Johnson Credo (their statement of shared values) allowed individuals to react swiftly during the Tylenol tampering incident without wasting valuable time on "chain of command" or seeking formal approval. Lower level managers made the decision to pull millions of dollars of suspect product off the shelves because that action was consistent with the company's long-held values.

JOHNSON & JOHNSON CREDO

- We believe our first responsibility is to the doctors, nurses and patients, to mothers, to fathers and all others who use our products and services.

- We are responsible to our employees, the men and women who work with us throughout the world.

- We are responsible to the communities in which we live and work and to the world community as well.

- Our final responsibility is to our stockholders. Business must make a sound profit.

Source: Excerpted from the Credo in Johnson & Johnson Press Kit.

Many organizations are beginning to recognize the power of shared values and make them part of their reward and recognition system. Jack Welch, CEO of GE, represents the new breed of corporate leader who passionately believes in the importance of the organization's values. In a recent interview, he stated:

> *"In an environment with values, everyone can create a win. Values are a key to our success at GE. Our first value for GE is to 'Create a clear, simple, reality-based, customer-focused vision and be able to communicate it straightforwardly to all constituencies.'"*

Behavioral Norms, Heroes and Organizational Systems

While it is difficult to see Values and Beliefs, it is easy to see their effects in the organization's behavioral norms, financial and Human Resource systems, the behavior of managers and employees, and "hero" stories. This is the visual part of culture and the behavioral norms can be seen in the style and pace of meetings, frequency and importance of planning sessions, work habits and hours, communications between different levels and functions of the organization, style of dress and office decoration, level of cooperation vs. competition. Values and Beliefs are also formalized into the organization's systems: personnel policies, procedures, rules, project review systems, budget approval policies and other systems.

Another way the organization's culture is displayed is through Hero Stories. The behaviors and actions that become "legend" within a company are strong indications of what the company believes is important. However, behavioral norms, organizational systems and hero stories are more than just the visible clues to the organization's culture. They also reinforce and perpetuate the culture.

People are shaped by the behavioral norms that surround them and guided by the systems created by the organization. The hero stories that are repeated to new members of an organization introduce them to the corporate culture. Some companies do this formally as a way of shaping behavior: Wal-Mart still actively promotes stories about Sam Walton as an example of positive Wal-Mart cultural values. Other organizations do it more informally such as many of the Silicon Valley companies that continue to tell stories about the "early days" and the creativity of founding heroes.

THE SECRETS OF RESHAPING CULTURE

Even when one accepts the fact that culture can make or break any change initiative (or any company for that matter), the question is, can culture be changed and if so, how?

Reshaping culture is similar to changing lifelong habits and behaviors of a person. It is not easy to stop smoking or permanently lose weight, but people do. It is not easy to break down the walls between departments, but organizations can become more boundary-less.

The good news is that more organizations are recognizing the need to shift culture, and are working at it. The bad news is, like losing weight, most companies make too little progress too slowly. Our research and experience has taught us what it takes to successfully reshape a culture and why most companies fail.

Rule #1
ORGANIZATIONS ARE SHADOWS OF THEIR LEADERS

We learned this lesson early in our history. J.L. Hudson, a division of the Dayton Hudson Corporation in Detroit, asked us to help them work on improving customer service in their stores in the late 70s. (To make them more like Nordstrom.) We piloted the process in six stores working with the store managers. We had mixed success. Some stores had measurable increases in service levels and increased market share, while others didn't. In fact, the results were almost directly proportional to our success in shifting the store manager's focus from operations to service, and his/her management style. It was as if the stores were a shadow of their leader.

We concluded our mixed success was a result of starting at the wrong level in the organization. We found this out in an interesting way. When we would ask sales associates why they weren't more attentive or friendlier to customers, they would in different ways say, "Who's friendly and attentive to me?" When we would ask their department managers the same question, we got the same answer. That continued on up through the assistant store manager, the store manager, the district manager, the vice president of stores, and on up to the executive committee. We concluded that "fixing the stores" was similar to family therapy, you have to include the parents. Later, when the CEO of The Broadway Department Stores in California asked if we would develop a customer service process for them, we politely said, only if we can begin with the executive committee. That led to several consecutive years of increased sales and market share for The Broadway.

All too often leaders in an organization will kick-off meetings about quality, but not develop quality measures or improvements in their own work. They will announce reengineering, but not reengineer their own jobs. They will approve of training programs dealing with changes such as culture, but not work on changing themselves.

Rule #2
YOU CAN'T CREATE WHAT YOU CAN'T DEFINE

No company would think of operating without an income statement, a balance sheet, or some sort of budgeting process. Those things define the quantitative goals for the organization, and let everyone know when they are on target. Yet, most organizations have no clear definition of culture and no way of measuring cultural ingredients. Detailed cultural definitions in the form of Values and Guiding Behaviors are a cornerstone of the change process.

Rule #3
DEFINE THE GAP

How much change is needed and in what areas? Not only do organizations have income statements, balance sheets and budgets, but they have variance reports and periodic audits to see if they are on target. Few companies do an effective job in auditing their culture and measuring the gap.

- What is the degree of change readiness?
- How deep is the resistance to change?
- How easy will it be to create cross-organizational solutions?
- Will the historical hierarchy and level consciousness prevent the use of competency-based vs. position-based teams?

Rule #4
GET AN OUTSIDE VIEW OF YOUR CULTURAL STRENGTHS
AND WEAKNESSES

There is an interesting saying that relates to culture, "We don't know who discovered water, but we're pretty sure it wasn't a fish." Understanding a culture is a similar phenomenon. It's like water to a fish, they don't know what it is because they are immersed in it. The same is true with corporate cultures. When people are surrounded by it everyday, they don't see it. It's like living in a noisy city, pretty soon you don't hear the traffic. This phenomenon has been referred to as "familiarity blindness" or "cultural trance."

Rule #5
CHANGE IS A FUNCTION OF PERCEIVED NEED

In a personal interview, Lee Iacocca described to us how and why Chrysler got serious about culture change.

"We bought American Motors, which was a big merger. We had to integrate them at the same time the market crashed 508 points. It all happened within two weeks. And that awakened us. And it didn't take six months to say, 'We're going to die if we don't change.'

"We had to change major habits in our culture. This country was built on the rugged individualism that characterized the 1930s, 40s, and 50s. Everything was top-down, as in the army or the Catholic Church—the great hierarchies of the world. The word comes down from above. That's the way the hierarchy of business was done. That's a tough culture to change. But easy or not you have to change. We did it at Chrysler. We began with off-site meetings, we now call 'Core

Sessions.' We started with our officers, and then we took the training down into the organization. We immersed our managers in the culture change."

Much of the resistance to change in companies today is because people in the organization don't see an compelling need for change and therefore don't have a sense of urgency. One client of ours, a large regional phone company established a "Competitive Newsletter." In it they printed every piece of news on how technology was changing and how others were moving to take their market. They went to great lengths to communicate that they could either shrink as an old-line phone company or get their costs and culture in line and be a winner in the new information age.

Rule #6
BEHAVIORAL CHANGE OCCURS AT THE EMOTIONAL,
NOT INTELLECTUAL LEVEL

Meaningful change in the beliefs, habits and behaviors of people often come as a result of significant emotional events. It rarely comes from reading a book or attending a lecture. Events like a health crisis, a divorce or the birth of a child, will cause someone to look at the world through a different set of "eyes." The same is true for organizations. IBM, Sears and other organizations are in the process of remaking themselves. This probably wouldn't be happening without the crisis they face.

Given the importance of crisis as a triggering activity, how does a company reshape its culture without a looming crisis? We have found that people can be drawn towards a positive vision of the future that is both compelling and emotionally rewarding. This is understandable in the light of the fact that deep-seated values and beliefs reside in the heart or the gut, not in the head.

Statements of values hang on the walls, but don't live in the hearts of employees because this rule is so often violated. We have found that unless a senior team arrives at their values through a specially designed team process, preferably an off-site retreat, which creates a positive, shared, emotional experience, they won't be internalized. Unless the values are internalized by the senior team, neither the understanding nor the commitment will be deep enough. Habits and culture can only be changed through an insightful, personal experience, not an intellectual seminar or lecture.

Rule #7
CULTURE CHANGE REQUIRES A
FEEDBACK-RICH COACHING ENVIRONMENT

Reinforcement is critical to behavior change. Annual reviews of performance are not adequate to support culture change. We've asked hundreds of groups of executives in our seminars if they receive enough useful appreciative or constructive feedback to help them with behavior change. Not once has a group said "yes."

In our off-site Executive Leadership Workshops, participants are often shocked to find that they receive more useful feedback that helps them improve their leadership skills during a 30 minute interactive exercise than they have in the past 5 to 10 years of their careers.

Culture Change requires day-to-day ongoing coaching where people are appreciated for new behaviors, and supportively and constructively coached when they are violating cultural conventions. In addition to active coaching, other more formal reinforcement mechanisms must be set in place.

Rule #8
LEADERSHIP SKILLS AND CULTURE CHANGE WORKS BEST
IN NATURAL WORK GROUPS

A few years ago we were asked to review the culture change efforts of a large corporation. It had spent millions in training and education and hadn't made a dent in the old hierarchical, command-and-control culture. Like many organizations, it had set up a sophisticated, in-house "university." They offered a wide variety of topical courses on leadership, teambuilding and culture, and they also sent selected executives off to some of the finer business school programs in the country.

The problem was, people that worked shoulder-to-shoulder on real issues rarely went to the classes together; therefore, they didn't have a common language nor were they able to reinforce one another's learning. Since leadership and coaching take place within the context of a team, team-based training is vital to culture change.

Some years back we were not effective enough in communicating the importance of this rule. Because one client had such serious turf issues, and because they historically had done their training by level of the organization, they began to roll-out trainings horizontally to mixed groups of employees, all at the same organizational levels. Later we found that they weren't applying the concepts enough on the job. Because intact work groups had not had the same shared bonding experience, they didn't feel permission to coach one another on new ways of working together. When we switched to intact team training to reconnect them, the culture change dramatically accelerated.

INTEGRATING REENGINEERING, PLANNING AND CULTURAL AWARENESS

By gaining a thorough understanding of corporate culture and its impact on performance, the senior management team, the reengineering core team, and the outside consulting group, can better use the levers of culture to support the reengineering process. At the same time, they can avoid the mistakes that tend to create resistance and other cultural barriers.

We recommend that very early in the reengineering process, the importance of culture change be discussed. In some form or another, the senior management team should get an "overview" on corporate culture and several open discussions should take place about the need to integrate an understanding of culture change into the reengineering process.

The company should seek out those firms that have already attempted culture change. Talk with the senior managers...listen to their experiences...meet with groups of employees... learn the power of culture to either support or block the change process. And don't just talk to those in your industry. This isn't benchmarking we're talking about here, it's learning, opening up to new ideas wherever they come from. It's getting excited about the possibilities that can happen in your organization!

In addition, it is important to begin to educate the entire

employee body about culture, the need for fundamental change in American business today, the need for change within our company, and the importance of culture in the overall change process. As much as possible, this should be a fact-based message, with a balance of both "potential threat" as well as "future opportunity." The danger of communicating the need for change using only the "fear of loss of jobs," is that it can often, especially in unempowered, more hierarchical cultures, drive employees into a "foxhole" mentality.

As one middle manager recently described it:

> *"For the past month all we've heard from senior management is WE need to change, or else! We hear lots about competition eating our lunch, how we are 'bloated' and not cost effective, how we've got to get rid of 'dead wood' employees who aren't pulling their weight! There's no opportunity in these messages, no picture for the future. As a result, it's easy to see why many employees have gotten into a 'hunker down' attitude where everybody tends to lie low, be as inconspicuous as possible, don't make any waves, and for certain don't volunteer for anything that could make you stand out as being one of the 'dead woods'!"*

While many talk of the negative impact of change, Maggie Murfitt from Rank Xerox UK, one of the members of the team that reengineered the order processing area, describes the positive aspect of change management:

> *"Working together (in action teams from across the company) has helped people see each others' points of view and also to appreciate the skills and qualities that they need to perform their jobs. The level of respect among the teams has really gone through the ceiling—everyone knows that they are working towards the same goals and that they are there to get the customer what he or she wants."*

It is also important to place a "culture expert" on the Reengineering Steering Committee that is being set up in

Phase I to guide the overall process. Culture, culture change, and cultural barriers should form an equal part of the agenda of every meeting of the steering committee.

Ensuring the Outcomes with Purpose and Empowerment

One of the most dramatic organizational changes we have seen was undertaken by Branch Banking & Trust Company (BB&T) of North Carolina, and led by its Chairman, John Allison. BB&T was a regional bank that was growing at 8% per year in a market that was growing 10%, and it was rapidly losing market share, as well as its own confidence. What did it take to turn the organization around to one that averaged over 31% growth per year for over five consecutive years? According to Allison, overcoming resistance is mostly being fanatical about getting everyone aligned around a clear purpose and empowering people at all levels.

Allison and the employees of BB&T found that the secret for overcoming resistance and building an entirely new organization was culture change:

- Get absolutely clear about your real purpose as a business.
- Achieve 100% buy-in to that Purpose.
- Empower employees at all levels to focus on Purpose, not just Goals.
- Eliminate, in a caring manner, the resistors.

According to Allison, this early experience of reengineering their organization had a profound and positive impact on his own personal life and the lives of all those employees who participated in the bank's purpose: "solving the financial problems of our customers."

Most senior managers forget that there is a basic conflict that occurs between Management and Employees that becomes accentuated during times of change. That conflict is a fundamental difference of focus between management's financial focus and most employees' customer focus. Employees don't get nearly as excited about cost reduction as they do about solving a customer's problem. And many managers forget that the bottom line numbers they look at everyday on spreadsheets come from the pockets of thousands of customers that they never interface with.

One of the major problems during change is that much of the focus of management gets intensified on the financial objectives, which adds to the feeling by employees that customers are going to get less service than before. These two different focuses are analogous to a pair of binoculars where each of the two eye pieces are focused on different scenes... it's easy to wind up with a splitting headache that way! Leaders of Change must understand that their job is not to try and make both focuses the same, but to tie them together, like the cross-pieces of steel in a good pair of binoculars that keep each of the eyepieces aligned. This is possible by developing a higher "purpose" that both groups can buy into.

BUILDING OBJECTIVES AND PURPOSE

A Culture Change Objective and a Reengineering Performance Objective should be developed early on in Phase I, and both should be expressed together with an overall Business Purpose Statement that will guide all employees through the entire process of change.

Reengineering Performance Objective	+	Culture Change Objective	+	Business Purpose Statement	=	100% Focus

A "Reengineering Performance Objective" should be developed based on the outcomes to the ultimate end user—the customer. An example could be:

> *"Through a dedicated application of the principles of reengineering, we will focus all our work activities on our customers in such a manner that our costs will be in the lowest quartile of our competitors, our quality will be in the top 10%, and our customer satisfaction ratings will be the highest in our industry."*

The "Culture Change Objective" should be a clear picture of the internal working environment during the reengineering process. An example could be:

"During this reengineering process, we will engage the energy, excitement, and ideas of all our employees in such a healthy manner as to have open, honest dialogue, empowerment, accountability, and teamwork become a part of our ongoing corporate culture."

The development of the "Business Purpose" statement is critical to providing human energy and aliveness to the entire change process. Everyone needs a Purpose to believe in. And very few of your employees will fully believe in and commit to "improved earnings per share" or "reduced costs and faster cycle time!" These are end results, not purposes. A purpose is something that gets people up in morning and makes them feel good during the day, not just when the results are in! Look for your Vision and Purpose statement in the things that really matter in your organization. For example, one of our clients, a toy manufacturer, expresses their Business Purpose Statement this way:

Making the world safer and even more fun for babies and children!

And the employees of BB&T expressed their overall "Purpose" as:

Solving the financial problems of our customers.

By framing and committing to a Reengineering Performance Objective, a Culture Change Objective, and then developing an overall Business Purpose Statement, the entire organization can identify with a balanced set of outcomes for the change process.

⌐ Reader Activity ══════════

Building Objectives and Purpose

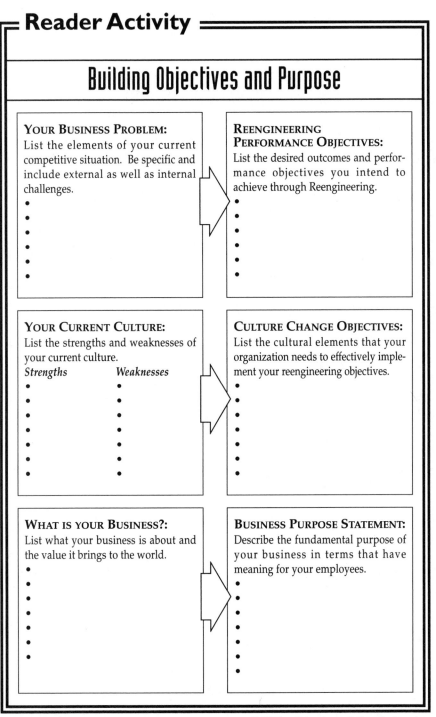

YOUR BUSINESS PROBLEM:
List the elements of your current competitive situation. Be specific and include external as well as internal challenges.
-
-
-
-
-
-

REENGINEERING PERFORMANCE OBJECTIVES:
List the desired outcomes and performance objectives you intend to achieve through Reengineering.
-
-
-
-
-

YOUR CURRENT CULTURE:
List the strengths and weaknesses of your current culture.

Strengths   *Weaknesses*
- 　　　　　　 •
- 　　　　　　 •
- 　　　　　　 •
- 　　　　　　 •
- 　　　　　　 •
- 　　　　　　 •
- 　　　　　　 •

CULTURE CHANGE OBJECTIVES:
List the cultural elements that your organization needs to effectively implement your reengineering objectives.
-
-
-
-
-
-

WHAT IS YOUR BUSINESS?:
List what your business is about and the value it brings to the world.
-
-
-
-
-
-
-

BUSINESS PURPOSE STATEMENT:
Describe the fundamental purpose of your business in terms that have meaning for your employees.
-
-
-
-
-

6

✸

PHASE II: CORPORATE CULTURE AUDIT

Without a clear picture of the current culture, it is impossible to understand the tremendous impact and influence that your organization's culture will have on the outcome of reengineering. Embarking upon any change initiative without understanding the strengths and weaknesses of the current corporate culture, is like pulling out of your driveway on that fabulous summer vacation you and the kids have been talking about all winter, but not checking the gas, oil level, or general workings of the car. It's a design to fail!

So how can we get a clear picture of our current corporate culture?

This is not easy, since the existing culture is often "invisible" to those working inside the company. The underlying values, beliefs, and even the norms and policies and procedures that make up the current culture are so commonplace that "cultural myopia" becomes real. Too often management aggressively defends "the way things are done around here" as being somehow perfect and certainly not a contributor to poor performance! The only way to determine the degree to which culture is a "Root Cause" contributor is to develop an objective picture of the current corporate culture.

Even though this may be difficult for insiders, there are a number of ways to get clues:

• *What gets attention in conversations and in meetings?* If, for example, 90% of a typical management meeting is spent talking about reducing costs, and 10% is spent on how the customers are feeling, then you probably have more of a cost-driven than a customer-driven culture.

• *Notice people's behavior.* If you were to make up a list of behaviors that you see frequently, whether the behavior contributes to or detracts from the good of the company, what would be on the list? For example, if people in your culture tend to shoot down new ideas, pointing out why they will not work, then that would be a characteristic of your culture. Or, if people in your culture tend to openly appreciate each other, then that would describe your culture.

• *What are the "hero stories?"* An equally influential part of the visible culture are "hero stories." The behaviors and actions that become legend within a company are strong signals of the way things should be done around here! Who do people stand around and talk about with pride and respect? What behaviors do these people exhibit? Who gets applauded at meetings? What are the behaviors that warrant the applause? Within all strong cultures the keen observer will find dozens of stories that clearly spell out the expectations the company has for its employees.

• *Ask "what if" questions.* In working with a large electric utility, we asked the senior team to imagine who in America could be their toughest competitor if they decided to go into their business, and how they would have to change to survive. The group picked Microsoft and Motorola and concluded that they would have to eliminate the bureaucracy, be far more open to change and have a markedly higher bias for action.

• *Get fresh feedback.* Check with those who have "stranger's eyes." Ask the newest managers in your organization to tell you what they notice in the culture that's different for them. Ask them to describe what they see . What did they first notice as strengths and challenges? Do the same with longtime trusted vendors and any consultants working on projects within the organization. All can provide outside perspective.

An additional and even more direct way to understand your current culture is to get assistance in conducting a corporate culture audit.

The Culture Audit

Culture audits basically take two forms: the "Subjective Interview Method," and the more objective "Questionnaire or Profile Method." Our recommendation is that both are important in gaining an understanding of a company's current culture. Together, they develop a more complete picture.

The interview methodology gives good rich information, filled with examples and feelings, but its subjective nature makes it hard to analyze or quantify the information. The quantifiable profile or questionnaire method delivers measurable data, but is without any real integrated meaning or contextual understanding. Together, however, they have a positive synergistic effect that helps paint a very complete and understandable picture of the strengths and weaknesses of the current culture.

While several "canned" profiles are available, it is advisable to develop one that is tailored for your organization. While the pre-packaged materials may be slicker and somewhat less time consuming to get completed, there is great value in developing, administering, and analyzing one tailored for you. Just by going through the process of deciding which questions to ask, the senior management team will learn about their corporate culture. And by implementing it, you will quickly learn the degree of openness, honesty, or self-confidence of your culture. And even more important than the "statistics," is the richness of the discussions that will occur as you work through the summary as a group.

Our recommendation is that an outside consultant, an expert in culture, be retained to help the company develop and implement their culture audit. In many cases they are the best ones to conduct the interview portions since in many cultures it is not necessarily "job healthy" to tell it like it is to insiders. And then of course there is the important area of confidentiality. An outside expert is also important when it comes to interpreting the information.

One incident with a client bears this out:

> As we were conducting a three-day off-site Senior Management Retreat, it became obvious to us that this was a very "unhealthy," typical male "club" culture. There were an unusually large number of sexist jokes and innuendoes, even with one woman as a member of the senior team. To look at them, many of the men were overweight, several smoked and drank excessively, didn't exercise, worked long hours, and were prone to angry outbursts. And they couldn't wait to get together and share the latest joke. Who inside a company is going to confront the "bosses" and point this out as an unhealthy part of the culture?

> As the consultants who had conducted the one-on-one interviews during the culture audit and helped this team develop the questions for a cultural profile, it was obvious to us that this was a real cultural issue that could easily act as a significant barrier during the upcoming reengineering process. When we brought it up, there was an immediate and vociferous denial, with such explanations as: "you consultants don't understand the stress of a real job; this is the way we unwind and keep our sanity around here! Besides, it's all in good fun, people understand that!"

> After standing our ground and gently feeding back to them what they were saying, one of the members of the team finally had the personal courage to stand and say: "I must admit that this has been bothering me for some time and I just didn't have the courage to say anything. This is no longer the 1950s, times have changed and people expect more respectful and values-based leadership from us. To be quite honest, my spouse is very concerned with my weight and health, and so am I!" Well, the flood gates burst and what ensued was one of the most honest and open discussions this group had ever had as a management team. A deep commitment developed that night that was to be the foundation for a significant culture-shift and a real jump-start for their reengineering efforts.

The story continues: About two weeks later, as we were working with the Chief Legal Counsel of the team, he turned to us and said: "You probably don't know that our company has been very close to two sexual harassment suits in the last few months and I've been scared to death that our behavior was going to lead to some major multi-million dollar lawsuits that could severely cripple this company. I think our discussion has really put an end to this old behavior and I want to thank you, both as the legal officer of this company, and as a person."

DEVELOPING A CULTURE AUDIT

Through an active process of one-on-one interviews with all levels of the organization, evaluation of current planning documents, assessment of existing HR policies, review of corporate history, and an understanding of the industry and its driving forces, it is possible to establish a profile of the current culture and its strengths and weaknesses.

In developing the questions and areas to explore, we recommend some of the following:

- What are the major strengths of this company?
- How well is this company prepared for the future?
- In what ways is this company vulnerable?
- Which areas in the organization tend to cooperate, and which ones don't?
- Is more effort spent on internal competition or external?
- When a goal or deadline is missed, or a result not accomplished, do people tend to make excuses and blame others or are they highly accountable?
- Is it OK to make a mistake around here?
- Does the organization tend to be hierarchical and level conscious?
- Do people tend to have a strong work ethic? Is there any stress and burn-out?
- What is our customer service really like?
- Does the culture tend to encourage new ideas or shoot them down?

- Are issues openly discussed in meetings or afterwards in the hall?
- What are the current levels of trust and openness in the organization?

Additional "informal" and subjective approaches are also helpful in assessing culture. In addition to those described earlier, it is helpful to:

- Disengage yourself from your own view of the business.
- Talk with employees with whom you would not normally interact.
- Ask your spouse for feedback about the company.
- Make a list of company jokes; there is usually more truth than humor in them.

An understanding of the behavioral and emotional elements of your current culture will help you gauge the potential degree of acceptance or resistance to change in your organization.

For example, at Columbia Gas Transmission, the reengineering team quickly became aware of a significant aspect of the culture: micromanagement by senior management which stifled creativity and initiative. It became readily apparent when Michael Casdorph, Senior Vice President and the overall head of the transmission company's reengineering project, interacted with the project team members. Mike's normal everyday approach, like many of the senior executives throughout the Columbia Gas System, was to be actively engaged in problem solving and daily work issues. That approach carried over to the reengineering team as well.

In an attempt to be helpful, again a Columbia Gas cultural trait, Mike would often walk into the conference rooms used by the reengineering teams, offer suggestions, direction, and provide "guidance." His very vocal style, coupled with the fact that the old culture was "top-down," made his "suggestions" more like "orders," and while the team expected this as normal senior executive behavior, it was not in the mold of the new working environment the team was trying to develop as a model for a culture that supported reengineering.

When this trait was brought to Mike's attention and he

openly held discussions with the team, he quickly began to recognize how his behavior and "old culture" approach to providing leadership and oversight were at odds with the concepts of empowerment of the reengineering process and the new culture needed. Mike also realized that in order for the reengineering recommendation to be a "team" recommendation, and not Mike's, a change in management style was required. As a result, Mike made a conscious effort to modify his style to one of support, providing resources, managing road blocks and coaching on individual issues when asked. Over a period of six to eight months, the team noticed a big difference and acknowledged to Mike that he was now displaying the elements of the new culture. Everyone saw that this new set of behaviors was more compatible with the reengineering process than the old cultural behaviors.

By conducting your own culture audit you should become clear about the strengths and weaknesses of your current culture. What cultural norms work for your organization? Against it? How could your current culture inhibit the reengineering process?

The answers to these questions will prepare the senior management team to begin an open and candid evaluation of the current culture and their role in leading the performance improvement process.

CORPORATE CULTURE PROFILE

One tool we have developed that is helpful in getting a handle on culture is the Senn-Delaney Leadership Corporate Culture Profile[SM]. A group, usually beginning with the entire senior team, is asked to complete the profile. They mark their perceptions of the strength of each of 18 cultural traits on a scale, such as the one shown on page103. The sample can be as small as the senior team or as large as the entire company. With one multi-national firm a Corporate Culture Profile was administered to a total of 1,000 employees from various levels in a dozen different countries.

The profiles shown in the following charts are representative of a large, United States company in the energy industry.

ABC Corporation Corporate Culture℠ Profile Output

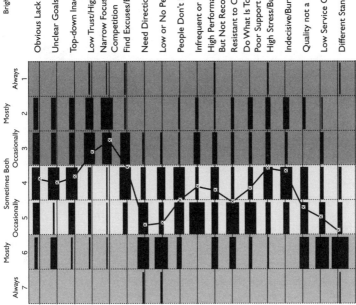

Number of respondents: Senior Executive Team (18)

Bright bars represent relative percentage of respondents who gave that rating.

Clear Alignment/Common Focus of Leadership at Top — Obvious Lack of Alignment at the Top
Clear Goals and Direction (Common Vision) — Unclear Goals and Direction (Confusion)
Two-Way Frequent Open Communications — Top-down Inadequate Communications
High Trust/Openness Between People — Low Trust/Highly Political
Teamwork/Mutual Support and Cooperation — Narrow Focus/My Area Only/High Internal Competition
People Take Accountability for Their Results — Find Excuses/Blame Others/Feel Victimized
Self Starters/High Initiative — Need Direction/Low Initiative
High Performance Expectations — Low or No Performance Expectations
People Feel Appreciated and Valued — People Don't Feel Appreciated and Valued
High Levels of Feedback on Job Performance — Infrequent or No Feedback on Job Performance
High Performance is Recognized and Rewarded — High Performance is Always "Expected" But Not Recognized
Open to Change — Resistant to Change
Encouraged to Innovate/Creativity Welcomed — Do What Is Told/Don't Rock Boat
Healthy/Fast-Paced Environment — Poor Support for New Ideas
Sense of Urgency/Bias for Action — High Stress/Burnout Pace
High Quality Awareness and Focus — Indecisive/Bureaucratic/Slow to Respond
High Service Consciousness/Focus on Customer — Quality not a High Priority
High Integrity When Dealing with Employees — Low Service Consciousness
— Different Standards for Different Levels

© 1995 Senn-Delaney Leadership Consulting Group, Inc.

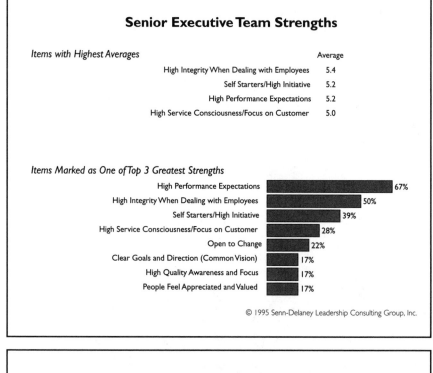

Senior Executive Team Strengths

Items with Highest Averages   Average

High Integrity When Dealing with Employees   5.4
Self Starters/High Initiative   5.2
High Performance Expectations   5.2
High Service Consciousness/Focus on Customer   5.0

Items Marked as One of Top 3 Greatest Strengths

High Performance Expectations — 67%
High Integrity When Dealing with Employees — 50%
Self Starters/High Initiative — 39%
High Service Consciousness/Focus on Customer — 28%
Open to Change — 22%
Clear Goals and Direction (Common Vision) — 17%
High Quality Awareness and Focus — 17%
People Feel Appreciated and Valued — 17%

Senior Executive Team Challenges

Items with Lowest Averages   Average

Narrow Focus/My Area Only/High Internal Competition   2.8
Low Trust/Highly Political   3.1
Find Excuses/Blame Others/Feel Victimized   3.6
High Stress/Burnout Pace   3.6
Indecisive/Bureaucratic/Slow to Respond   3.7
Top-down Inadequate Communications   3.8

Items Marked as One of Top 3 "Most Need to Improve"

Narrow Focus/My Area Only/High Internal Competition — 56%
Low Trust/Highly Political — 50%
Obvious Lack of Alignment at the Top — 44%
Indecisive/Bureaucratic/Slow to Respond — 39%
Unclear Goals and Direction (Confusion) — 33%
Find Excuses/Blame Others/Feel Victimized — 28%
Top-down Inadequate Communications — 22%
Do What Is Told/Don't Rock Boat/Poor Support for New Ideas — 11%

The strengths are obvious. They are a high integrity company of self-starters with high-performance expectations. They genuinely care about customers and service. The lowest scores are indicative of a regulated utility "mind-set": internally competitive, highly political, and bureaucratic. This company is struggling with change caused by deregulation and increasing competition, but so far has done an ineffective job of communicating to their employees why they need to change, and after considerable downsizing, trust levels are low. It is interesting to note that this company is at the front end of a major reengineering process and already they are encountering difficulties because of resistance to change, interdepartmental turf issues, and power struggles among division leaders.

The data from the culture assessment interviews and the corporate culture profile was convincing enough evidence to management that they decided to move more aggressively on reshaping their culture to support their reengineering initiatives.

Reader Activity

Culture and Its Implications for Reengineering

List the key strengths and weaknesses of your current culture as indicated in your culture profile. With your senior team, determine the possible implications these can have on the reengineering process.

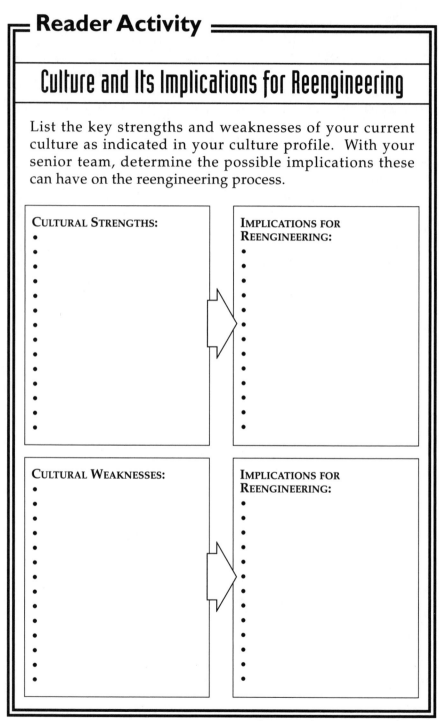

CULTURAL STRENGTHS:
-
-
-
-
-
-
-
-
-
-
-
-
-
-

IMPLICATIONS FOR REENGINEERING:
-
-
-
-
-
-
-
-
-
-
-
-
-

CULTURAL WEAKNESSES:
-
-
-
-
-
-
-
-
-
-
-
-
-
-

IMPLICATIONS FOR REENGINEERING:
-
-
-
-
-
-
-
-
-
-
-
-
-

7

PHASE III: BEGIN AT THE TOP

At age 66 Stanley Gault accepted the challenge of turning Goodyear Tire & Rubber around for a reason that was "98% emotional." Because Goodyear is the last major American-owned tire company, Gault was willing to devote three years of his life to rebuilding the company. He commented in an interview with Fortune magazine:

> "We needed a tremendous cultural change involving everyone in the organization. When you're in this kind of jam, time is not on your side."

One of Gault's first actions was to clarify the future objectives for the company. Using film and television, he transmitted his message worldwide in a way that allowed everyone to see how they fit into the picture...no one was excluded. At the same time they discontinued using the word "employee" in favor of the term "associate."

After the term "associate" started gaining acceptance, three or four mill workers approached Gault after a meeting and one of them asked hesitantly if the word "associate" applied to him. Gault states, "Well, I tell you, that really grabs you, doesn't it, when this guy with 35 years of service...wants to know if the word "associate" applied to him." Gault assured the worker that he was an associate and made a special point to visit the area where he worked. Through the grapevine and e-mail, his actions were transmitted around the world "in 60 seconds" according to Gault.

THE SHADOW OF THE LEADER

> "A leader doesn't just get the message across—a leader is the message."
>
> —Warren Bennis

What leaders do is as important, perhaps even more so, as what they say. Effective leaders shape the culture of their organizations through a powerful combination of message matched by action. Through their actions, attitudes and messages, they cast a shadow that influences everyone around them, in the workplace, at home and in the community.

The shadows of great leaders extend far beyond their own lives. John Fitzgerald Kennedy's actions and messages called for commitment and involvement. Part of his legacy is the Peace Corps and the conquest of space. Mahatma Ghandi and Martin Luther King, Jr. advocated, and demonstrated, non-violence and their non-violent protests of existing conditions changed the world as we know it.

But, the shadow of the leader is not limited to world leaders. Business leaders, teachers, parents, church and community leaders all cast a shadow that influences others. In very meaningful ways, hourly employees who interact with customers are "leaders" who cast powerful shadows about the company and its real commitment to service. Actions that match the message make the shadow longer, influencing people much more powerfully. Actions that vary from the stated messages or company slogans also demonstrate what's important, and not always in ways that add to the "bottom line."

The following organizational charts tell the story of "shadow of the leader":

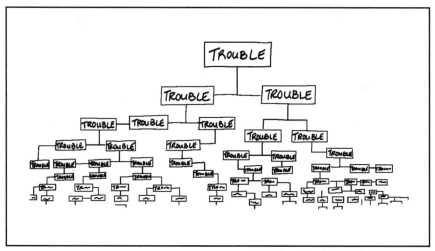

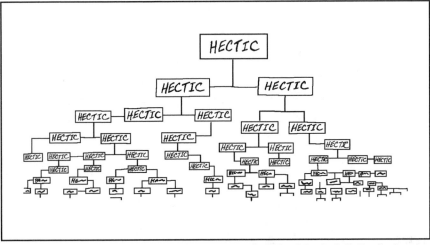

One of the most intimate and far-reaching examples of this shadow concept happens when parents, perhaps aware of their own imperfections, exhort their children to "Do as I say, not as I do." Unfortunately, children generally tune out that message and mimic the behaviors they see. James Baldwin states,

> *"Children have never been very good at listening to their elders, but they have never failed to imitate them."*

The message of any parent or business leader will be drowned out if the actions conflict with the words.

One of our favorite songs from the 60s is good wisdom for parents and corporate executives alike:

Children Learn What They Live

If children live with criticism, they learn to condemn.
If children live with hostility, they learn to fight.
If children live with ridicule, they learn to be shy.
If children live with shame, they learn to feel guilty.
If children live with tolerance, they learn to be patient.
If children live with encouragement, they learn confidence.
If children live with praise, they learn to appreciate.
If children live with fairness, they learn justice.

If children live with security, they learn to have faith.

If children live with approval, they learn to like themselves.

If children live with acceptance and friendship, they learn to find love in the world.

Parenting is a huge responsibility and too often we forget how our behaviors and attitudes affect our children. Henry Wheeler Shaw once said: *To bring up a child in the way he should go, travel that way yourself once in a while.*

The role of the leader, at work and at home, requires modeling the desired behavior, letting others see the desired values in action. To become effective leaders, we must become aware of our shadow and then learn to have our actions match our message.

One way to better understand the impact that leadership has upon employees is to make just a little shift in the above poem, then as you read it, picture your organization and your leadership shadow:

Employees Learn From Their Leaders

If employees live with criticism, they learn to blame others.

If employees live with hostility, they learn to resist.

If employees live with ridicule, they learn to avoid risks.

If employees live with shame, they learn to underestimate their abilities.

If employees live with tolerance, they learn to learn.

If employees live with encouragement, they learn confidence.

If employees live with praise, they learn to appreciate.

If employees live with fairness, they learn accountability.

If employees live with opportunity, they learn to have faith.

If employees live with approval, they learn to like themselves.

If employees live with acceptance and recognition, they learn to find fulfillment in the workplace.

Warren Deakins, President and CEO of Fidelity Mutual Life Insurance Company feels strongly about the importance of consistency between actions and words and states:

> *"I would submit to you that it is unnatural for you to come in late and for your people to come in early. I think it is unnatural for you to be dishonest and your people to be honest. I think it is unnatural for you to not handle your finances well and then to expect your people to handle theirs well. In all these simple things, I think you have to set the standard."*

The head of an organization or even a department casts a shadow that influences the employees in that group. The shadow may be weak or powerful but it always exists. It is a reflection of everything the leader does and says. Marjorie M. Blanchard, President of Blanchard Training and Development, Inc. describes it this way:

> *"People are smart. If you say one thing and do another, people see the discrepancies. Every decision I make as a leader in my company is being watched for the meaning and the values behind it. When you make a mistake, you create a negative story that can last a long time. So leaders have to lead by example, and be aware of the impact they create."* (Source: *21st Century Leadership. Copyright 1993 by LINC Corporation and Senn-Delaney Leadership Consulting Group, Inc.)*

Entire corporations often take on aspects of the personality of the senior executive. For instance, Microsoft is known for being innovative and competitive...a direct reflection of Bill Gates; while Wal-Mart's culture of being friendly, thrifty, and customer-focused comes straight from its founder, the late Sam Walton.

Sometimes corporate cultures are so closely connected to the leader of the organization that it is almost impossible to think of the organization without thinking of the leader as well—Herb Kelleher at Southwest Airlines, Lee Iacocca at Chrysler, Fred Smith at Federal Express, Walt Disney and the Disney companies. This is the power of the shadow in action; the power to shape and influence the outcome for the organization.

Cultural Implications of the Shadow of the Leader

One of the most common complaints we hear throughout organizations is that the senior team is "not walking the talk." Whenever a company begins to make statements about desired behaviors and people don't see those behaviors being modeled at the top, there is a sense of lack of integrity. This can take various forms:

- The organization is asking people to be more open to change and the top leaders are not themselves changing.

- Increased teamwork and cross-organizational collaboration is preached and the senior team itself is not a good team.

- The organization is seen to cut back on expenses and the senior team doesn't change any of its special "perks".

- People are being asked to be accountable for results while the senior team members continue to subtly blame one another for lack of results.

We have found that the fastest way to create a positive self-fulfilling prophecy about cultural change is to have the leaders individually and collectively shift their own behaviors. They don't have to be perfect, they just have to clearly deal themselves into the same game.

Our years of observing this phenomenon have led us to conclude that culture-shifting initiatives will be successful only if the senior team itself formally engages in a process of changing their own behaviors. When leadership, teambuilding, culture-shaping trainings are a part of the change process, the senior team should be the first team that takes part. If 360° feedback instruments are to be used to measure behaviors, then the senior team should be the first to step up and be measured.

Anyone who has ever worked with training processes with middle management knows their limitations. When attendees are asked about the value of the session, the classic responses are, "my boss is the one who should be attending" or "it sounds great but that's not the way it is around here, just ask my manager."

Because of the critical need for the senior team to role model (shadow) the new culture, they are the group that needs to come together in a shared, off-site process to define the guiding behaviors for the organization. Whenever this is delegated to a committee under them or to expert writers, the statements of values may read well, but are not owned by and don't reside in the hearts of the senior team. When they don't "live" in the senior team, the probability that the organization will live the values is low.

As a firm that specializes in the area of culture-shaping, we have an unwritten policy that unless we are doing something as a demonstration or pilot project, we won't design and conduct culture-shaping sessions for clients unless we can work with the CEO and the senior team. It is not that we would not like the business, it's just that we know that it is unlikely to work.

Leading Reengineering

The same phenomenon of Shadow of the Leader impacts reengineering. For the process of reshaping an organization through reengineering, the actions and behaviors of the leader(s) of the organization are a critical factor in the overall success or failure of the improvement efforts. It is easy to see how a CEO, or even a key department head, can bring a reengineering effort to a sudden halt, just by a few words spoken in the heat of frustration, or by withdrawing funds for the process when sales decline.

Jamie Houghton of Corning Inc. provides an excellent example of how enlightened, dedicated leadership can transform a company. At the time he assumed the CEO position of Corning in 1983, the company was a classic example of a "rust belt" organization. Almost 70 percent of the company's business was in mature cyclical markets and profits had declined for the past three years. In addition, Corning held small to modest market shares in its core businesses.

Jamie Houghton brought a focus and sense of urgency to the company. In the same year that he assumed the CEO role he announced his plan to spend $5 million on the overall objective of "complete customer satisfaction." The company's employees and management were not impressed. Having been through many superficial improvement programs, they believed this was just another "flavor of the month." To combat this, Houghton demonstrated real commitment to the new vision. He appointed the company's first Director of Quality and established a goal of five percent of employees' time devoted to training. He and his corporate management committee were the first graduates of the two-day training course. He established recognition programs such as the Houghton Award, given annually to the division with the most effective customer satisfaction program. He demonstrated his personal commitment by becoming a tireless champion of customer satisfaction throughout the company — meeting with over 50 employee groups yearly. In the words of one employee "his message has never varied in the past 10 years."

To drive the customer focus down through the organization he established the "Vital Few." These are the measurements of each division's products and services that are most important to its customers. Each division's performance on its Vital Few measures is tracked regularly by Houghton and the management committee. Progress against these measures is also graphically exhibited throughout the company so that employees are given continual feedback on their performance. The company's reward systems were modified to support the new version with a percent of each employees' salary and bonus being impacted by performance on the Vital Few. In addition, communication and employee opinion is solicited by a number of mechanisms such as internal customer satisfaction assessments.

All of this activity has transformed the culture of the company. The number of corrective action suggestions by employees has risen from 800 per year before Houghton assumed leadership to over 16,000 per year currently. There are now over 2,000 problem-solving teams working on corrective action programs. These results have also impacted the company's bottom line.

Return on equity, which stood at 7.3% in 1983 was at 14.1% in 1994. Defects at a ceramic production unit were reduced from 10,000 parts per million to 3 parts per million. On-time delivery at its clinical lab testing unit went from 88% to 98.5%. At another unit, customers' deadline for quotes was missed a full 50% of the time before Houghton's programs were instituted. Now 100% of the quotes are received by the customer on-time every time.

Jamie Houghton exhibited vision, commitment and dedication in his mission to transform the culture at Corning. He has led by example, never letting up over the past 12 years.

The same kind of dedicated, mission-oriented, maniacal leadership that makes a turnaround possible is just what is needed during a reengineering effort. Lip-service or superficial support won't work because people will be watching the leader very closely for any sign of wavering or conditional support. Since reengineering is about massive change that can be intensely threatening and unsettling, it is critical that the leader cast a shadow of complete commitment.

A committed leader can be the single most powerful force for successful reengineering. Blue Cross and Blue Shield of the National Capital Area recently underwent a process improvement initiative in their claims processing and customer service operations, one of the largest areas in the company. The initiative resulted in cost/headcount reductions of over 30% and reorganized six departments into one. The overall leader was Alice Morehouse, Vice President of Operations, who understood that she had to demonstrate to all employees that change was possible and everyone needed to be a part of the process, including herself. She was willing to show her commitment to personal and organizational change through her active involvement with Action Teams and by removing obstacles that impeded progress.

Alice demonstrated her commitment to creative change through employee involvement, mutual respect, accountability and continuous improvement by forming Action Teams with all levels of associates. These Teams were empowered to solve problems, develop recommendations, and implement solutions. Initially there was resistance to change, and a disbelief that the Teams could be successful at all levels of the organization. The teams also had to overcome a number of cultural obstacles to make the process improvement a success. Claims processors were deciding what tools they needed to better do their jobs. This was a new role for the claims processors and a change for middle management, who now had to respond to their requests. One tool they needed was a phone on their desks. Trusting the claims processors not to abuse the phone was a cultural change toward empowerment, accountability and efficiency for all levels of the company.

Alice worked with the Teams to break down entrenched beliefs regarding the work, as well as roles and abilities of the staff. Change may often be resisted, but as Alice found, success is probable when there is clear respect and involvement of all parties.

In many ways the success of any reengineering initiative is strongly dependent upon the commitment, skills, attitude and style of senior management. Thus the reengineering effort naturally begins at the top and the reengineering process becomes a "shadow" of the leaders. It is important for the top management team to spend time together forming the basis of the new culture. Until senior management has identified the cultural barriers that need to be removed and are committed to removing those barriers, reengineering changes will not be taken seriously at lower levels of the organization.

BUILDING AN ALIGNED LEADERSHIP TEAM

High-performance, aligned teams do not just happen, even if you have been able to select the "best people for the job!" Real teams are developed, not assembled, as any basketball or other sports fan can tell you. Having the best talent doesn't mean they will play well together! Achieving the teamwork and alignment necessary to build a high-performance culture is an important task that must be accomplished before the reengineering effort can really get underway with momentum and credibility.

Building and maintaining an aligned, high-performance management team is the job of the leader. In many ways, he or she is the "team leader," coach, and manager, as well as a player and member of the team. After 16 years of designing and conducting senior executive teambuilding sessions for Fortune 1000 Corporations, we have witnessed firsthand the changes that can happen in the culture and performance of an organization by having a real "team at the top."

The most effective senior executive leadership, teambuilding, and alignment processes combine business realities with interpersonal dynamics in such a manner as to develop a new, fresh set of behaviors at the top, and point them at the key business challenges. Our experience has been that executive retreats that focus entirely on the business challenges are valuable at identifying the issues, but unless the team is already aligned and working very well together, interpersonal barriers can stymie good business plans. On the contrary, sessions focusing solely on interpersonal skills can be personally useful, but without putting the learning in the context of the company's business situation, less than effective positive change in the business will occur. From such sessions one often hears: "I really feel closer to my team now, but how do we apply this good feeling to our business problems?"

When reengineering is the issue, many of the senior executive retreats we design for clients are three days in length and tend to focus on the theme of "Building Leadership Alignment to Support Reengineering." These are highly interactive workshops where each day's activities tend to prepare the group to go further and deeper the following day.

Having experienced a three-day Senior Executive Leadership and Alignment Retreat for his leadership team, Ray Smith, Chairman and CEO of Bell Atlantic remarked:

> *"My senior management team and I had to first look at ourselves, our personal beliefs, and our management style built up over the years. We had to come together and forge a new set of shared values, a new level of teamwork and leadership."*

A COMMITMENT TO REENGINEERING

Here are a few of the leadership "shadows" critical for a successful reengineering effort:

- HOW MUCH TIME SHOULD WE DEVOTE TO REENGINEERING?

One of the key indicators of the "commitment" of top management to reengineering is the amount of time they give to the process. Everyone knows that "top management must show their support," but what does that really mean in terms of time? While reengineering is still a young concept and very little data exists, a McKinsey study of nine companies and their reengineering activities showed that in those cases where senior management spent 20–60% of their time devoted to the process, the results were "right on target," as opposed to those where there was a low commitment from senior management (Source: Hall, Eugene A., Rosenthal, James and Wade, Judy. *How to Make Reengineering Work.* in the McKinsey Quarterly, 1994, No. 2)

"20–60% of my time? Are you people crazy?"

CEOs and senior executives with that attitude should think twice about embarking upon a reengineering effort. Without committed leadership, the odds run strongly against success! If having up to half of the CEO's time spent on the reengineering effort seems excessive, remember the enormous potential payoff of reengineering efforts which can be ground down by the "jaws" of corporate culture! The radical changes required by reengineering will not happen unless employees see the need for change and the benefit of change. They will not willingly disrupt their work lives unless they believe that the effort has a chance of succeeding...and that requires the total commitment and support of senior management. People not only need to hear the words, they need to see the CEO (and the senior management team) down in their work areas, encouraging, supporting, listening, carrying the vision, and pointing out the benefits of a successful effort.

"OK!! OK!! But what are we going to be doing during all that time?"

In one word...COMMUNICATE. Communicate the vision. Communicate the commitment. Share information. Pass along success stories from other organizations and from other areas within the organization. Bring the customer to life for every employee in the organization. Listen. Ask questions. Ask for ideas and suggestions. Provide feedback, both appreciative and constructive. Celebrate wins.

In two words...COMMUNICATE and DEMONSTRATE. Demonstrate the new cultural values. Become part of the team. Be available. Stress cooperation between functions and departments. Stimulate new ideas. Focus on adding value to customers. Show respect to everyone in the organization. Support new ways of doing things.

- ALLOCATION OF RESOURCES

Almost nothing speaks louder in an organization than the allocation of resources. What's the real budget for this reengineering stuff? Are the best people assigned to the project or is it a resting place for misfits? Are the necessary tools and facilities available? Resource allocation is a major indicator of leadership's dedication to a change initiative. Reengineering efforts demand the best people available and allocation of anyone less than the best blasts a signal through the organization that cannot be overcome with nice speeches and memos.

> *"You're asking me to put Bob on that project? But he's the best operations manager we have in that region. We need him in the field!"*

What's the message? Field operations (today's processes) are more important than the reengineering project (tomorrow's streamlined processes).

- ENSURING THAT REENGINEERING IS DRIVEN BY CORPORATE STRATEGY

There is no greater role for senior management during reengineering or culture change than to ensure that the process is driven by the overall corporate strategy. This is not about change for change sake. This is about competitive advantage, customer focus, increasing shareholder value, developing organizational capabilities. Strategy is the driver. The entire reengineering team, as well as the whole organization, must understand that we are undertaking these changes because it is strategically imperative. Throughout the communication efforts of senior management, this one theme must be hammered home again and again.

8

PHASE IV: DESIGNING A HIGH-PERFORMANCE CULTURE

The Ford Taurus is the best-selling car in America and the Ford Explorer set the standard for the now popular Sport Utility Vehicles. Before Ford could create these incredible wins, they had to address enormous cultural barriers. The old Ford culture supported a stifling bureaucracy that virtually eliminated creativity. The tendency toward empire building created departments that were insulated and competed with each other for resources. Ethical concerns were virtually ignored and the prime emphasis was on looking good internally. Needless to say, the company had lost touch with its market.

Donald Peterson was committed to changing that negative culture and with it Ford's future. During his ten year tenure (1980–1990) as President and then Chairman of the Ford Motor Company, Peterson focused on creating a shared vision and set of high-performance values for the company, with two of those key values being Total Quality and Customer Focus. With a great deal of persistence and leadership, the company shifted its old culture to one that displayed innovation, teamwork and a close connection with customers.

The exceptional performance of companies with strong values is thoroughly discussed in the book, *Corporate Culture and Performance,* by John P. Kotter and James L. Heskett. In this important research work following numerous companies over a ten year period, they convincingly state:

> *"Organizations that give more than lip service to mission statements, stressing the values of people, are more likely to have effective performance because managers feel energized and willing to help the firm change with the competitive environment."*

The values that members of an organization share create a template for corporate and individual behavior. When these values have been clearly stated and accepted by all members of the organization, they set guidelines and standards for making decisions, determining priorities, solving problems, and addressing competitive pressures.

The flip-side of a high-performance culture with healthy shared values is a culture whose values are vague and fragmented and whose culture seems to put up barriers whenever the organization tries to change.

A HIGH-PERFORMANCE CULTURE

> *"Our job is to provide a culture in which people can flourish and reach their dreams—in which they can be all they want to be."*

—Jack Welch

All cultures are different and there is no one "perfect" culture just as there is no one perfect personality. While there is no perfect corporate culture, it seems that organizations which possess healthy, high-performance cultures all have a similar feeling about them. In some of our recent senior executive retreats for U.S. corporations, we have been asking them to describe what a high-performance culture would be like. Remarkably, they all tended to come up with a similar feeling and even some of the same words. Many described a high-performance culture this way:

> *It would be flexible and highly adaptive...where employees display a "can do" attitude, a contagious sense of optimism and belief in themselves and their products and services, and where people at all levels feel energized, motivated, and find that they are growing both personally and professionally by being a part of the company. A high-performance culture sees business and people problems as part of the game and tend to keep a healthy perspective and balance between numbers, results, people and relationships. Everyone has a focus on the customer, knows what is important, where the company is going, and can't wait to beat the pants off the competition.*

One manager in a recent workshop described it this way: *"There's a lightness here that makes working long hours seem energizing instead of stressful and tiresome!"*

Sound ideal?
Sound impossible?
Worth having?

High-performance organizations do exist, but they don't happen by accident, nor without visionary and committed leadership. During our research for the book *21st Century Leadership*, the kinds of winning shared values the leaders mentioned repeatedly included:

- Integrity and honesty
- Empowering leadership
- Openness and trust
- Teamwork and mutual support
- Caring
- Openness to change
- Quality, service and a customer focus
- Respect for the individual and for diversity
- Winning and being the best
- Innovation
- Personal accountability
- A "can-do" attitude
- Balance in life

As a result of our work we have also compiled a list of the most common cultural barriers and their corresponding winning behaviors.

CULTURAL BARRIERS VS. WINNING BEHAVIORS

Cultural Barriers	*Winning Behaviors*
• Hierarchical leadership	• Empowering leadership
• Turf issues	• Teamwork and mutual support
• Opportunism and lack of principles	• Ethics and integrity
• Hidden agendas, dishonesty and lack of openness	• Open, honest and flowing communication
• Distrust and fear	• Trust
• Short-term and strictly bottom-line driven	• Long-term quality, service and excellence
• Task-oriented and internally focused	• Customer/market-oriented and externally focused
• "Can't be done" attitude	• "Can-do" spirit
• Blame and making excuses	• Personal responsibility and accountability
• Co-dependence and excessive independence	• Interdependence
• Prejudiced and judgmental	• Embracing diversity and differences
• Insufficient training	• Continuous learning and knowledge development
• Stress and burn-out	• Focus and balance
• Holding onto the past and resisting change	• Innovation, ingenuity and breakthroughs
• Strict rules and rigid policies	• Flexible, fluid and rapidly responsive
• Win/Lose games	• Win/Win games and bigger wins for entire organization
• Boss driven	• Coaching—appreciative and constructive feedback

Core Values in High-Performance Cultures

While companies have distinct cultures, we have found that there is an amazing similarity in terms of core values in successful organizations. It's almost as if there are a set of principles of organizational effectiveness which are akin to principles of life effectiveness for people. While they are stated in different ways, combined in different ways, and prioritized in different ways, the list in one form or another includes the following elements:

- integrity
- openness and trust
- respect for the individual
- personal accountability and empowerment
- openness to change and innovation
- feedback and coaching
- teamwork

These are often personalized or emphasized in different ways. Welch talks about "unyielding integrity, a boundary-less organization" and "relishing change." A pharmaceutical client dependent upon new innovative products uses a phrase, "trailblazing" to represent innovation and change. An insurance client, Mutual of Omaha, substitutes the word "solution seekers" for "accountability" and a CEO of a savings and loan used "relentless drive for improvement."

Foundation Values

The purpose of values is to provide a road map for behaviors in the organization. Three of the values are what might be called foundation values (Figure 8.1). While they by themselves don't ensure results, without them an organization is crippled. Those are:

- Ethics and Integrity
  - Mutual Respect
    - Openness and Trust

Any great edifice will last only as long as the foundation that supports it. Similarly, high-performance cultures must be built upon a solid foundation of Ethics and Integrity, Mutual Respect, and Openness and Trust. Without these three foundation principles firmly in place in the hearts, minds, and policies of the leaders and employees, attempts to create a new culture that will draw out all the creative energies and ideas of its people will be wasted.

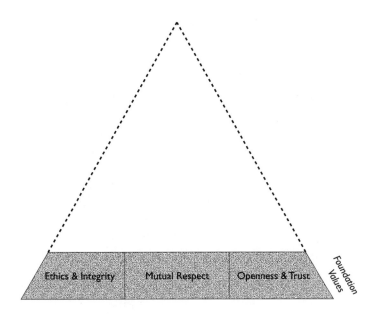

Figure 8.1

• ETHICS AND INTEGRITY

"Integrity is not a 90 percent thing, not a 95 percent thing; either you have it or you don't."

—Peter Scotese, retired CEO, Spring Industries

We have found in our work on values with dozens of organizations, that most leaders, when talking about values, emphasize ethics and integrity as as a foundation value.

Unless the bedrock of a leader's life, or an organization or a government is built on integrity, instability will ensue. As David Kearns, former Chairman and CEO of Xerox Corporation, said, " It's absolutely imperative that we have a cadre of people coming up into the leadership core that really understand the issue of integrity."

Ethics and integrity are a cornerstone of all high-performance cultures. The word "integrity" implies consistency or congruence between words and deeds, while "ethics" suggests a system of moral standards that an organization or individual uses to guide decisions and daily behaviors. The most common elements of ethics and integrity are: honesty, fairness, compassion and social responsibility.

While virtually all businesses speak highly of the need for integrity, and pride themselves on being models of modern business Integrity, a deeper examination of the meaning of the word reveals that today's "definitions" are somewhat lacking. Integrity draws from the same root as the word "integer."

A person of high integrity is not only honest, he or she also sends a single and singular message of being one person and of one mind on an issue. This is manifested in many ways including: not speaking different messages to different audiences, not talking out of the side of one's mouth, practicing what one preaches, walking the talk, or getting the "hips" to move in the same direction as the "lips." Texans traditionally refer to integrity with a clarity that draws from their heritage: "Don't write a check with your mouth that your body can't cash!"

Leaders involved in reengineering and other major change activities soon learn that not honoring verbal commitments is a failing in "integrity" in the eyes of employees. This awareness, when combined with the process of reengineering, can have profound impact on how the process of reengineering is presented and managed. Speeches and communications with employees take on a new sense of seriousness in an effort not to violate their "integrity" by saying something about the process, like hedging on the job elimination questions, since it quickly weakens the foundation of the entire process.

Leadership-by-example is an imperative for high-performance cultures. Leaders must demonstrate consistency between message and behavior...they must "walk their talk." High-performance cultures generally develop a code of ethics that clearly spells out behavioral expectations for the organization and its members. This code is used as the basis for spreading an increased level of candor throughout the culture so that honesty and fairness become the normal way of interacting. This code creates a clear sense of "right and wrong" and establishes a line that is not to be crossed. That doesn't mean that the organization isn't aggressive or competitive but it does mean that the organization's actions are consistent with its values. John D. Macomber, while Chairman and President of Export-Import Bank of the United States, put it this way: "Great companies have always walked on a high ethical, moral plane."

• MUTUAL RESPECT

"You build a team when you consider the well-being of each person on your team."

—Sanford "Sandy" McDonnell, Chairman Emeritus
of McDonnell Douglas Corporation

In today's business environment, employees differ greatly in gender, race, ethnic background, and age. Being able to deal with the many issues of diversity is fundamental to organizational performance. Many experts on diversity and its impact on organizational performance strongly believe that unless Mutual Respect is firmly imbedded in the corporate culture, diversity training and other programs will fail to make positive inroads.

Mutual respect in organizations is easier to see than to define. Its essence lies in the way we treat others and the way we design our policies and organizational systems. The elements of mutual respect include human resource fundamentals such as pay and benefits, but goes well beyond them to reflect a recognition of the importance of every individual to the organization. It includes pleasant, functional working spaces, open access to other members of the organization regardless of rank or position, a sharing of information and rewards, a high level of training and development, and involvement in the planning of work processes.

Mutual respect is often reflected in terms such as "associates" or "partners" instead of workers or employees. Mutual respect assumes that each person in the organization is capable and well-meaning. Rather than trying to control individual actions, the high-performance culture concentrates on creating an environment where people can function at their highest levels.

• OPENNESS AND TRUST

"Trust is the key value of our times."

—James E. Burke, former Chairman
of Johnson & Johnson

When employees believe that the organization and its leaders are ethical and have integrity and there is an atmosphere of mutual respect, it is possible to create an environment of openness and trust. This environment is open to new ideas, honest communication and different points of view. It promotes feedback—both appreciative and constructive—which facilitates problem identification and solution. Conversely, environments that do not have open, honest communications tend to preclude new ideas and change—because of the possibility of failure, and therefore criticism.

John Allison, Chairman of BB&T Financial, an outstanding performing regional bank based in North Carolina, has led the transformation of his organization from a laggard to a star, using a fierce belief in people, purpose and trust.

"You have to be serious about trust. Most businesses do not trust their employees. Trust is a personal thing. I literally trust everyone that works for me. They are not perfect, but that is different. I do trust them. Absolutely and completely. I trust everybody I work with. If you do not trust them, chances are, they do not trust you."

In an open and trusting environment, employees at all levels are encouraged to "tell it like it is," challenge old ways of doing things, bring up new ideas and focus on solutions and possibilities. This type of candid and open environment can only occur when people have trust and are able to separate the person from the behavior or actions.

Performance Values

While values like integrity, trust and respect provide a sound foundation for an organization, they do not ensure success. What is it that separates the winners from the losers? It is not only the skills, competencies and foundation values, but a specific mind-set of individuals and teams that makes the difference. The critical performance values we've identified include:

- Teamwork
- Personal Accountability and Empowerment
- An Openness to Change
- A Commitment to Continuous Learning and Personal Growth through Coaching (Figure 8.2)

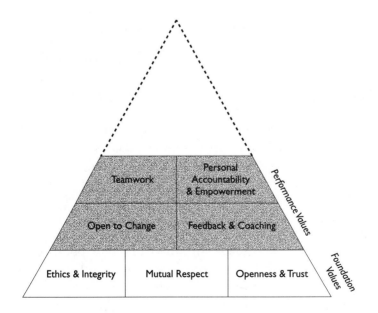

Figure 8.2

- TEAMWORK

"When teamwork kicks in, nobody can beat you."

—Don Shula, Head Coach, Miami Dolphins
(the only NFL team to attain a perfect 17–0 season)

Today's complex business environment requires interdependence of individuals and departments. Reengineering, which focuses on horizontal processes that cut across all parts of the company, requires people to work together in ways not required previously. In a high-performance culture, teamwork replaces individualism and competition between departments. The essence of teamwork is the belief and understanding that all people in the organization belong to the same team and must work together to achieve the overall goals. It's the understanding that, "I don't succeed unless and until the entire team succeeds."

An effective team is a group of people acting together in an atmosphere of trust and accountability who agree that the best way to achieve a common goal is to cooperate!

The ability to develop and lead good teams is the number one leadership skill required in today's organizations. Downsizing, "right-sizing," reorganizing, and reengineering are all indications of the pressure on organizations to reduce the costs of doing business in today's highly competitive environment. This often leaves departments and work groups with the same (or more) work to do with fewer people. Teamwork is not just a "nice to have," it is a requirement for success.

Reengineering, Total Quality Improvement, superior customer service, and other forms of improving competitiveness are all based on good teamwork principles. Without teamwork these improvement efforts generally end in frustration and even alienation.

The lack of teamwork can be extremely expensive. We have seen competing internal groups spending millions of dollars in time and external consultants trying to prove another division or function wrong. This extreme competitiveness often results in the withholding of critical information from a competing group, regardless of the damage to the entire organization.

Jon Katzenbach of McKinsey & Company and co-author of *The Wisdom of Teams,* speaks about teamwork with real passion. When asked the question of why team training is so popular, he replies: "Because teams produce extra performance results. There is virtually no environment in which teams—if done right—can't have a measurable impact on the performance of an organization."

While these benefits are critical to the success of an organization, there is also a set of softer benefits of teamwork which greatly enhance the working environment:

- Teamwork fills the real human need for socialization.
- People learn from each other in a team environment.
- Working together for a common goal is both motivating and provides a real sense of purpose and fulfillment.

• ACCOUNTABILITY AND EMPOWERMENT

"For the last two decades, the most exercised part of the corporate body has been the pointed finger!"

—Tom Peters

Many of our culture change clients term "accountability" the **make it happen** ingredient! Georgette Mosbacher, a successful business owner and author, was asked how she climbed from poverty and obscurity to the heights of corporate success. She replied:

"I know I can't be a winner and a whiner at the same time. And I choose to be a winner."

When individuals understand personal accountability and the fact that by their actions they can positively influence almost any situation, they become a key ingredient in the high-performance organization.

"Don't Blame Me!" How many times have you heard that statement uttered in anguish inside an organization? In the book, *A Nation of Victims,* author Charles J. Sykes, points to the decline in American competitiveness as well as an erosion in our quality of life as being linked to a general feeling of lack of control, a sense of having no power over events or circumstances. Sykes refers to this as "the victimization of America." He references a series of magazine articles that highlight this sense of victimization:

- *New York* Magazine—"The New Culture of Victimization—Don't Blame Me!")
- *Time*—"Crybabies: Eternal Victims"
- *Esquire*—"A Confederacy of Complainers"
- *Harpers*—"Victims All?"

Victim attitudes abound in organizations: blaming, excuses, "CYA" activities, "it's not my job," "it's not in the policy manual," and hundreds of other behaviors and attitudes which people use as a shield against taking risk and accepting their own personal accountability. These negative attitudes directly impact productivity, efficiency and the bottom-line.

However, accountability attitudes are also present in organizations. Without them, nothing would ever get accomplished. Some teams and organizations overcome enormous obstacles with their tremendous sense of personal and organizational accountability.

Accountability is the belief that an individual's actions (or inactions) are the major determinant of success or lack of success. Accountable people believe that they have a great deal of control over their own destiny and use their ability to make choices as their greatest tool for influencing outcomes and creating results.

"Choice, not chance, determines destiny."

Most people and organizations display both victim and accountability attributes—sometimes they are a role model of accountability and other times they play the victim. People can enhance their personal accountability while shedding nonproductive victim attitudes by increasing their awareness of accountability and recognizing their ability to choose the attitudes that are most productive for them.

People with a point of view of personal accountability tend to look for the "choice points" present in every situation. They know that by being aware of all the clues, they can determine the best choices that will most positively influence the outcome. When a situation doesn't go well, they ask themselves a lot of questions about why things didn't turn out the way they expected. And, they look first at their own actions, asking such questions as the following:

- What clues didn't I see?
- What extra steps could I have taken?
- What actions did I avoid?
- What should I have known?
- Who should I have confronted sooner?
- What personality traits or habits of mine might have aggravated this situation?

While it is true that the higher the level of personal accountability the better the overall outcome, it is not humanly possible to be 100% accountable all of the time. Expecting that kind of accountability from yourself or employees is not realistic, and often creates a great deal of negative pressure in which results start to dramatically suffer.

Where do accountable individuals draw the line when there is almost always more that could be done? The answer to this seemingly endless pursuit of perfection lies in the Serenity Prayer attributed to American theologian Reinhold Niebuhr:

"Grant me the serenity to accept the things I cannot change, the courage to change the things I can, and the wisdom to know the difference."

An underlying theme of every performance improvement approach is the involvement and development of people...or empowerment. An environment that fosters the growth and involvement of all employees creates the raw material needed to produce greater productivity, process improvement, and innovation. Empowerment means that people are more involved in the design of their work and in the decisions that affect them. As a result, they feel more ownership in the process and more committed to achieving the objectives.

Bill Gates, CEO of Microsoft, has led one of the world's most remarkable high-growth companies of this century. He describes empowerment as a necessary skill of leadership:

> *"As we look ahead into the next century, leaders will be those who empower others...Empowering leadership means bringing out the energy and capabilities that people have, and getting them to work together in a way they wouldn't do otherwise. That requires that they see the positive impact they can have and sense the opportunities."*

Empowerment means different things to different people. One definition we heard recently from an executive of a major company defined empowerment in the following way: *Real empowerment is telling people the goal, giving them the tools to do it, and leaving them alone.*

While many people would agree with this definition, we believe that "real empowerment" goes much further. The kind of empowerment that creates exceptional results is made up of two major elements:

> ...the letting go of tight controls by leadership
> and the acceptance of personal accountability by all employees.

This broader definition depends on letting go by management and the development of skills and confidence by the employee to capably handle added responsibility. Organizations with a clear vision and a high level of individual responsibility can multiply the eyes, ears and imaginations producing results. Empowerment simply releases more resources and creates more fulfillment and ownership.

The foundation of empowerment is an understanding that by getting people involved in all aspects of their work, they will perform better in the long run and be more committed to the organization. In a culture of empowerment, the organization's systems, policies and management behaviors encourage decisions by individuals and teams.

However, empowerment, employee involvement or participative management alone, without additional elements of responsibility, trust and respect, will not be effective. Before empowerment can be effective, individuals must have a mind-set of personal accountability. In a high-performance organization of accountability and empowerment, the work environment seems "turbocharged."

A common error often made is in the area of empowerment. While there's no question that a healthy culture promotes empowerment, companies can't mandate empowerment. In fact when organizations make broad statements about empowering their people, it often backfires. When people who feel victimized by downsizing and change are told that they are going to be empowered, it provides fertile ground for added victim statements. "I'm not empowered, you won't give me the budget." "I'm not empowered, you didn't let me make that change." While empowerment is an important value, it is often best to not state it explicitly. Instead the focus should be on personal accountability and a "can-do" attitude which is "self-empowerment."

> *"Empowered people believe that they make significant changes in the world around them. When you have that philosophy, there's nothing that can't be done."*
>
> —Barbara Levy Kipper,
> Chairman of Chas. Levy Company

- OPEN TO CHANGE

> *"Whenever you face a steepening slope of change, that is the time when you especially need wise leadership."*
>
> —Bernadine Healy, Director of National
> Institutes of Health

Never before have organizations been required to shift so dramatically to encompass such a variety of capabilities and talents in order to succeed. A key challenge now facing all leaders is how to effectively master the art of change. Change is not easy, especially with the habits built up from our previous paradigms of leadership.

Change comes in many dimensions. It includes a personal willingness to be open to continuous self-examination and introspection. One large corporation we studied was headed by a leader who talked almost exclusively about the past—the good old days. It was through this and other ways he signalled that he had stopped growing and the organization was feeling the effects. People who embrace change recognize that reaching ones' potential as a leader or a person is a journey— not a destination.

Another dimension of change is a persons' ability to be an effective change agent by learning to introduce change and lead it. In today's fast moving business world, a change agent is someone who invites and fuels innovation and looks for ways to improve everything. A third dimension is seeing "possibilities" in new ideas. One of the traditional beliefs about being a leader is, "If I'm shown a new idea, my job is to figure out what's wrong with it." This is what we learned and practiced in "management-by-exception." We are taught to be what we call an "observer-critic;" someone who challenges new ideas, plays devil's advocate, and tries to find inconsistencies. In this new era of change, it is important that cultures and people develop an openness that embraces change.

• FEEDBACK AND COACHING

> *"Personally, I'm always ready to learn, though I do not always like being taught."*
>
> —Winston Churchill

In this time of unprecedented change, the world demands a continuous level of improvement: shorter lead times, increased productivity, new skills, new products, new services, better communication, ever higher and higher levels of mastery. For companies to be effective in this rapidly changing environment, their leaders need to understand what motivates the people around them, as well as themselves.

For years the theory of motivation revolved around the "carrot and the stick." Managers were taught that motivating people was a matter of rewarding them for good actions and punishing them for bad actions. In organizations that use this theory, people spend most of their time avoiding the stick. As margins continue to shrink in our current business environment, the traditional "carrots" of promotions and raises become harder to afford and justify. This leaves people with little to work for and magnifies their motivation to avoid the stick by taking few risks and doing only what is necessary.

We now know that human motivation is much more complex than the simplistic idea of the carrot and stick; people respond to a variety of things. The following list was prepared by Rick Maurer in his book *Caught in the Middle:*

- **Meaning**—people want to know that what they are doing is important to the company or organization they work for. They also want to know that somehow, no matter how remote the connection, they are "making the world a better place." They want to "make a difference."

- **Results**—people like to see the results of their efforts. There's a sense of accomplishment and fulfillment that comes from successfully completing a task. Seeing the results of their efforts gives people a way to measure their progress.

- **Challenge**—people want to learn and grow. They progress by doing new things that make them stretch and develop new skills and capabilities.

- **Respect and Recognition**—people want acknowledgment for the things they do well. Recognition can be as simple as a pat on the back or as elaborate as a formal awards ceremony. An environment of respect and dignity gives everyone a foundation for performing their best efforts.

- **Control**—People want to have some say in the decision-making process. They want to be involved in what happens to them and around them; they want to feel empowered.

While motivation differs from person to person, Maurer's list is probably consistent with what most people want and also basically describes a coaching environment. This atmosphere creates the conditions necessary for people to do their best and feel good about what they are doing. The important characteristics of the coaching environment include:

- a caring and supportive climate;
- a coaching mentality among leaders;
- constructive feedback requested and given freely at all levels; and
- a balance of appreciation and constructive input.

Appreciation is probably the simplest and least-expensive method of motivating and rewarding people. Saying thanks, putting Post-it notes on paychecks, posting complimentary letters from customers, and celebrating outstanding efforts are simple, inexpensive ways to let people know they are appreciated and valued.

Just as important as expressing appreciation for work well done is providing constructive feedback on how to improve performance. All employees want to know how to do their jobs better. Studies show that most employees feel they do not receive enough coaching and feedback. Because they don't know how they're doing, they don't know what to change in order to improve.

A high-performance organization is one in which individuals encourage each other to expand their knowledge, increase their productivity and reach their potential. Employees see one important part of their job descriptions as "coach." The coach helps people become winners who reach their peak performance. A healthy, growth-oriented work environment is one that is "feedback rich." It provides the information people need to continuously improve their performance.

Adding Meaning to Core Values: Defining Guiding Behaviors

A professed value such as teamwork is not specific enough to define peoples' behaviors. To some it might mean being a good team player in their department, to others it might mean being a team contributor to the broader organization. Personal accountability to one person might mean doing my own job well and no more, while to others it might mean looking for any ways that they can contribute to the overall success of the organization.

We've been asked on many occasions to look at why culture-shaping initiatives are not working, even though a company may have written values. What we find is that there are a wide variety of interpretations of what those values mean. We have concluded that it's critical in the culture-shaping process to very explicitly define each Core Value with a set of Guiding Behaviors that clearly define the behaviors appropriate for that value.

An example of the way we define teamwork at Senn-Delaney Leadership via guiding behaviors is shown below:

TEAMWORK—GUIDING BEHAVIORS

1. Acts for the long-term benefit of the company even when it may take away from short-term personal benefits.
2. Develops positive working relationships with peers and others.
3. Supports fellow teammates to succeed.
4. Involves others in discussing issues and resolving conflicts.
5. Acknowledges others who demonstrate teamwork.
6. Informs and involves teammates whenever possible.
7. Seeks win/win solutions.
8. Shares information and resources with others.
9. Credits others for their contributions.

© 1995 Senn-Delaney Leadership Consulting Group, Inc.

As you can see, teamwork goes beyond being willing to cooperate. In this definition it requires someone to not be territorial, but in fact be willing to sacrifice individual or departmental goals in order to accomplish a bigger win for the overall organization.

Guiding behaviors also allow a company to much more specifically define the unique differences and the priorities in their own culture. They also provide some flexibility in terms of how many categories of values are needed since, for example, respect for individuals could be a guiding behavior under teamwork, and creative thinking or innovation could be under embracing change.

Guiding behaviors do one other critical thing for the organization, they provide a very specific list of observable behaviors that can become the foundation of a human resources reinforcement system, including performance appraisals, 360° feedback, and hiring and firing criteria.

VISION: THE DIRECTIONAL PRINCIPLE FOR PURPOSE AND MEANING

While values and guiding behaviors can describe how people operate within an organization, more is needed to provide the "fire" and energy needed for today's corporations to compete in the highly competitive global marketplace. That energizing factor is Vision.

> *"Vision is extremely valuable for rallying the spirit, feeling, and commitment of our people."*
>
> —John Pepper, President of The Procter
> & Gamble Company

At the very top of the high-performance pyramid is Vision (Figure 8.3). It is the capstone that brings the organization together, without which it is an incomplete structure without purpose.

> *"Where there is no vision, the people will perish."*
>
> —Proverbs 29:18

We use the metaphor of the operation of a bicycle. The rear wheel, like the culture, provides the power for forward movement. The front wheel, like vision, mission and strategy, directs the bicycle along the right path.

High-performance organizations combine a compelling vision of the future, a clear set of strategies and a high-performance culture.

Vision is the magnetic force that unleashes the drive, energy, creativity and courage needed to reach an objective. Compelling visions have empowered and released human and organizational potential throughout history. The powerful vision of a land where people were equal and able to control their own destinies allowed the fledgling American colony to wrest freedom from the much larger, better-financed British crown.

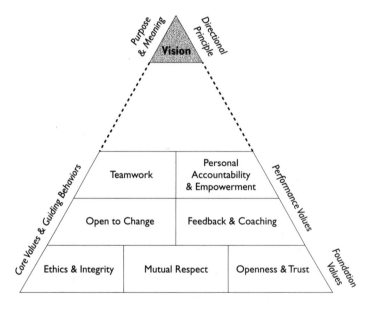

Figure 8.3

The vision of a man walking on the moon set into motion an enormous effort combining government, industry and educational institutions and changed our perception of the universe forever. The vision of change driven by a computer that could be used by anyone and everyone led a small group of Apple Computer employees to develop the Macintosh—a computer that set a new standard for ease of use and accessibility.

In human endeavors, thought precedes action. We have to know where we're going in order to get there. The more clearly we can "see" the final destination and the more we want to be there, the more energy we will have to overcome any obstacles in our path. A compelling Vision consists of two elements: a future-state that captures our imagination and a passionate desire to reach it.

Vision is a primary ingredient of success, whether by an individual, a team, a company, or a country. It's impossible to wake up one morning and say, "I'm going to be a success," and have it happen. You need to be a success at something. Only when the vision is clearly defined, does the path to success reveal itself.

In many ways, a clear vision represents "magnetic north" for employees within a high-performance organization. It represents the idealized picture of what the company and its employees can become. A vision is much more than just an objective or picture of a future; it evokes strong feelings. It is the feeling, not the objective, that tends to infect employees with high energy and commitment.

Vision imparts a clear picture of who we are, where we are going, and why it is important to us. Vision appeals to the more noble, cause-oriented elements within all human beings, and as such, unleashes creative energies, and uplifts the spirits of employees throughout the organization. Vision transforms strategies and missions into a "way of life" and significantly narrows the gap between plans on paper and forceful actions in the competitive marketplace.

Many companies make the common mistake of equating a mission statement and a vision. In a sense, they believe that goal setting and strategic planning are the same as visioning. While mission and strategy spell out the "how to's" in a company's quest for competitive advantage, vision is the "why to's" that motivate people to give their best with enthusiasm and commitment. People do not spring out of bed in the morning shouting: "Oh, boy, another day of earnings per share;" but they arise early and stay late to fulfill their vision.

Just as President Kennedy used the vision of a "man on the moon within the decade" to unleash the creativity of the nation to conquer the obstacles of manned space flight, so numerous businesses, even whole industries, have been built by the inspiring power of a vision.

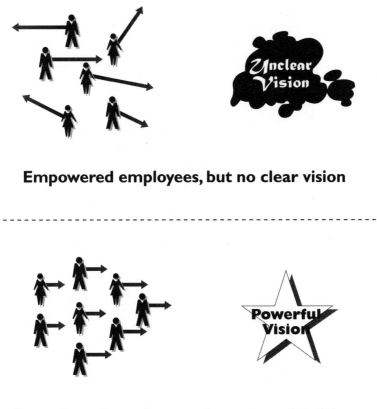

Empowered employees, but no clear vision

- -

Empowered employees; clear, powerful vision

The automobile industry, virtually non-existent at the beginning of the 20th Century, was pulled into being by the vision of Henry Ford to "provide safe, reliable transportation for the common man!" The modern telecommunications industry, which touches every part of our business and personal lives, gathered strength from the vision of Theodore Vail for a phone in every home and a commitment to "universal service, end to end." The photography industry is now a world-wide, multibillion dollar business, but its founding organization, the Eastman Kodak Company, "began with the vision of one man who saw a way to meet a very special need: The need to picture, share, and preserve the times, people, places, and events of our lives!"

When consulting business leaders on vision, we have found a number of universal themes that resonate with most people because they touch a core deep inside them. The first is a vision that improves the quality of life. For example, Bill Gates, Chairman and CEO of Microsoft, stated that his vision is, "to put a PC on everyone's desk." This vision, when achieved, will make people more effective and improve their lives. A second universal vision is to serve people in some way, for example, by having the best service, or providing exceptional value. The third is to be a part of an excellent, winning team. People will mobilize around a vision that calls for being the best at what they do. A well stated vision for an organization plays the same role as purpose does for an individual, both are motivational and directional.

Our own Vision has guided the growth and development of the Senn-Delaney Leadership Consulting Group for the past 16 years:

"Making a Difference Through Leadership"

"We are a high-performance team, committed to making a difference in the lives of people, the effectiveness of teams, and the spirit and performance of organizations!"

Principles for Alignment

While an energizing Vision and a set of Core Values and Guiding Behaviors define the subjective elements of business success, a healthy culture with unclear strategies and a poor competitive focus is a design to fail in today's fast-paced global marketplace. Now that we have a high-performance culture, what do we focus it on? A Vision is compelling and energizing, but not specific enough to determine capital allocations or budgets. A clear business mission and goals are needed (Figure 8.4).

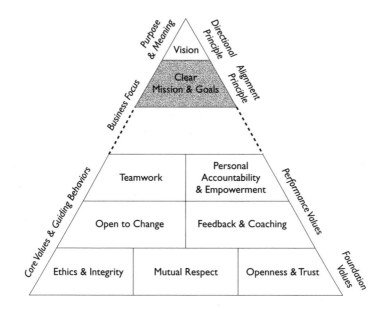

Figure 8.4

• CLEAR MISSION AND GOALS

"If you don't know where you are going, every road will get you nowhere!"

—Henry Kissinger

People want and need a clear path to follow. They need to know where the organization is going and what they're trying to accomplish. Without a clear mission and goals, every person in the organization is determining their own path. Some organizations follow a cow path through the woods, but high-performance organizations are aligned and speed along a superhighway that is clearly defined.

Effective organizations communicate the mission and goals to everyone in the organization so that everyone's going the same direction, working for the same objectives.

General Electric Power Generation is a highly focused organization that is achieving excellent financial results in a rapidly changing industry whose changes and increased competitive pressures have made it difficult for many organizations to survive. One of the reasons for the success of GE Power Generation is its focus on a clear mission and goals.

Our Mission	Be Recognized as the World's Leader in the Supply of Power Generation Equipment, Services and Systems
Our Commitments	Provide Our Customers with Products and Services of Such Excellence that GEPG is their Natural Choice
	Create an Environment Where all Employees Can Make a Difference and Grow to Their Full Potential
	Provide an Attractive Return to Our GE Shareholders on their Investments in our Business
	Behave as a Socially Responsible Member of the Communities in Which We Operate

Key Business Objectives

• Set the Industry Standard of Excellence for *Customer Satisfaction*
• Achieve *Total Quality*
• Maintain Clear *Technology Leadership*
• *Market Share Leadership* through a Market-Back Focus on Customer Needs
• Meet Business and Financial *Commitments*

These goals and the mission are so important to the company that all employees have "pocket cards" with the Mission and Goals printed on them which they carry with them throughout their daily activities at work. The pocket cards serve as a reminder of the importance of the mission, and are also used in meetings as a reference for day-to-day decision-making.

PRINCIPLES FOR COMPETITIVE SUCCESS

"Quality and customer service are our greatest competitive advantage for the next century."

—Kenneth Chenault, American Express

Having a culture that supports people, creates empowered teams with good coaching and feedback skills is important, but not sufficient for success in today's competitive marketplace.

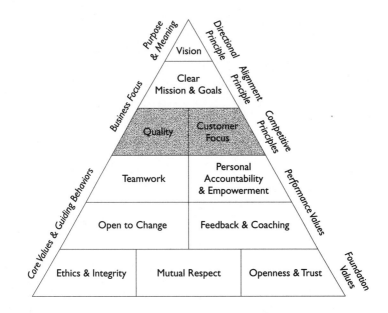

Figure 8.5

The best internal working environment, with a misdirected business strategy, is an invitation to disaster.

Most organizations now realize that quality and customer service are the two most effective long-term strategies for doing business in today's competitive, rapidly changing global economy. "Meeting or exceeding customer expectations" is common language in high-performance organizations.

There are two strategic principles that typify all high-performance organizations…an obsessive concern for quality and an unending focus on customer satisfaction. Success in the market place requires adherence to these principles (Figure 8.5).

- Customer Focus
  - Quality

One of the understandable debates that goes on with most teams working on culture is "Where does our focus on the customer and on quality fit? Is customer focus one of our values, or do we incorporate it in our vision and mission?" As with most debates in the subjective realm, there is no right answer. Some companies focus their vision on the customer, and then the values and the guiding behaviors define how they are going to achieve that. Others highlight customer focus as a key value of the organization, while for some, because of its importance, it's included in both places. However it is handled, it is a key part of the overall model of a high-performance organization.

• CUSTOMER FOCUS

"The purpose of a business is to create and keep a customer."

—Theodore Levitt, *The Marketing Imagination*

Everything else aside, there's only one player in the game of business who holds the money...the customer. And customers vote with their dollars. Businesses are voted in or out of existence by their ability to create value for the customer— value the customer will trade dollars for.

High-performance companies listen to their customers extensively. Market research is a constant, broad-based activity, not just the domain of one department. In high-performance companies, customers are a real presence to everyone in the organization: customers are pictured with the product, letters from customers are posted, front-line workers visit customer sites, customer-focus groups are conducted throughout the organization. The organization continuously talks about what the customer wants, when they want it and how much they will pay for it.

In the Corning Employee Handbook on Quality, Jamie Houghton, CEO, has put his thoughts down about how important a customer focus is on the survival of the company. The following is an excerpt from this material:

CUSTOMERS: WHO'S ON FIRST?

In the not-too-distant past most corporations treated customers as an annoyance at best. The only service customers could count on was "lip." Today's customers aren't passive recipients of goods and services. They want quality products and services, and they give their business accordingly. They come to the table with expectations and requirements.

At Corning, customers are valued partners in the business. We're focusing the company on customer results by providing our employees with the tools to help them measure and meet those customer expectations. We're also providing special support for our own front line soldiers: the customer service representatives.

All in all, it's turning the traditional organizational pyramid on its ear. And that's just fine with us.

• QUALITY

"Regardless of the exact definition, quality and satisfaction are determined ultimately by the customer's perception of a total product's value or service relative to its competition."

—Ronald M. Fortuna, Ernst & Young

Quality balances customer service with cost. It's an equation that constantly fluctuates as competing companies become more effective at meeting the needs of their customers. One competitor announces a new model or category of service and the equation shifts. Another competitor lowers prices and again the balance shifts. Still another competitor improves quality and the perception of value changes. High-performance companies are constantly striving to maximize the value equation by improving quality, reducing cost and giving better service.

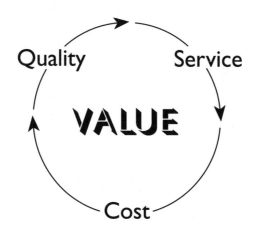

The story of how Xerox won the Malcolm Baldrige Quality Award really began in 1982 when Xerox was on the verge of going out of business. Under the leadership of David Kearns, the top 25 senior officers "signed up" for creating a high-performance culture founded on quality. The first decision to be made was "What is Quality?" In a week-long off-site workshop, they defined quality as "meeting customer requirements." That meant knowing what those requirements were and meeting them 100 percent of the time.

In turning Xerox into a fierce competitor in the copier and document creation and transmission marketplace, reviving the fortunes of the company, and winning the Malcolm Baldrige Award, Kearns and his senior management team went beyond the short-term objective of quarterly returns and put into place a key strategic principle in creating a high-performance culture that will deliver high levels of shareholder returns for years to come.

PRINCIPLES FOR ORGANIZATIONAL HEALTH

Our recent work on further strengthening the culture of our own firm has led us to conclude that there is a **sub-foundation** to high-performance cultures. This deeper foundation is based upon principles for organizational health, and includes the state of mind or moods of individuals and the organization, plus the ability of people to be present in the moment, rather than focusing on the past or the future.

- Moods
  - Be Here Now

- MOODS AND STATES OF MIND

Have you ever tried to give or receive coaching and feedback when you were irritated, angry or generally in a bad mood? How well did that work? Chances are not as well as if you had used a respectful and supportive tone.

We can be a better team player, coach, be more accountable, be more open and accept change better when we are in higher "states of mind." Our "state of mind" often takes the form of *moods* (see Figure 8.6), which move from high to low, much like an elevator. While part of the normal human condition, our moods have great implications. Some people not only ride the elevator, but get off and seem to fully furnish the lower floors, including defensiveness, blame and judgment. At a business meeting a group tries to explore issues or make decisions while at the lower mood levels and wonder why their meetings are so draining and few conclusions are reached.

An important question is what is, "normal" in the organization? Is frustration, unhealthy conflict, or high stress a way of life? Even unhealthy states can become "normal" to us and therefore become "invisible." It's much like living alongside a freeway for a few months and no longer noticing the noise or the fumes.

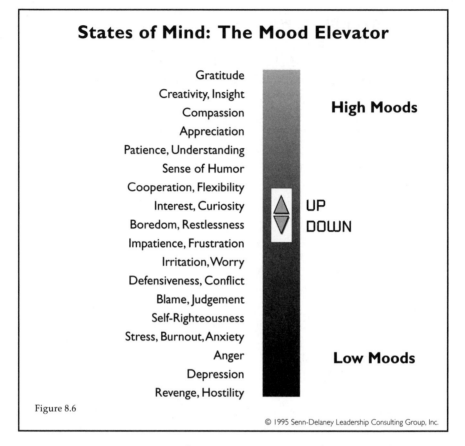

Figure 8.6

© 1995 Senn-Delaney Leadership Consulting Group, Inc.

Anytime we are at the lower levels of the mood elevator such as: irritated, angry, judgmental, or resentful, we don't do as well at openness, teamwork, accountability, coaching, change, or any of the other values or guiding behaviors.

Here are some hints to keep in mind that can minimize the adverse affects of lower mood states.

1.   By being conscious of our current mood, we can be more effective, because we can adjust.

2.   When on the lower levels of the mood elevator, remember that thoughts are usually unreliable. We have a tendency to misinterpret events and actions of others and see them in a negative light.

3.   Be aware that in the lower states we are not as effective at such things as coaching, collaboration, decision making, and problem solving.

4.   Utilize the thoughts expressed earlier in the serenity prayer. The less energy we waste in worrying about what we cannot change or being resentful of "what is" the better our state of mind will be.

5.   Keep things in perspective. When we are in a bad mood or in a low state things that bother us can be all-consuming. We can become "gripped" by them. Generally, if we look at the bigger picture in our total life including our health, our loved ones, our other accomplishments, or our life beyond work, things can be put into better perspective.

• BE HERE NOW

There is a particular state of mind that almost automatically puts people in the higher moods. It is a focus-on-the-moment we simply call: *Be Here Now.*

"He who lives in the present lives in eternity."

—Ludwig Wittgenstein

It happens every day—two people have a conversation but one of them isn't mentally there. A meeting is held but the participants are concerned about other issues. A manager goes home but continues to worry about the office. When people are doing one thing while thinking about something else, they are not really focused on either activity and both suffer.

The consequences of not being present in the moment are far reaching. An overactive "busy mind" creates an internal noise level that interferes with creativity and the ability to tap into the reflective, intuitive part of the mind. When our mind is cluttered, we can't really focus on what another person is saying; therefore, we don't really hear them and, consequently, they don't feel heard or respected.

When we can't turn off our whirlpool of thoughts, the quality of both work and home life suffer because we can give neither our full attention. The inability to leave work at work affects our relationships with our loved ones and keeps our batteries from being recharged by a restful, loving home life. This prevents our being fully effective at work.

The ability to focus and concentrate on what you are doing right now, what we call Be Here Now, is a critical skill for maximizing personal effectiveness and fulfillment. With our rapidly changing world and its uncertainty, the importance of balance and focus is more critical than ever.

Gary Mack, a well known sports consultant and team counselor, teaches professional baseball players to "breathe and focus!" A full mind, says Gary, equals an empty bat! When a spinning baseball approaches at 95 miles per hour, the batter needs all his focus on the present moment. Any thoughts outside of the present will leave the player standing as the ball goes by.

Some of the many benefits of "being here now" include:

- Increased productivity and quality when we focus 100% of our efforts on a task and avoid distractions.

- Better balance of personal and professional life—if we can be 100% present when we're at home and 100% present when we're at work, then we will have a rich, nourishing, fulfilling experience in both places.

- Easier, more fulfilling relationships—when people feel listened to and appreciated, they more easily develop deep, committed relationships. With a higher level of commitment and sense of self-worth, they produce their best efforts.

- Less stress, more peace of mind—worries about the past or concerns about the future create stress and reduce our peace of mind. In order to quiet our minds, we need to realize that the past is history and cannot be changed and the future is yet to be and will be determined by the choices and actions of today.

A Balanced High-Performance Culture

A more complete pyramid of organizational effectiveness would therefore look like Figure 8.7. Attention should be paid not only to the values and vision, but also to the state of mind of individuals and the organization.

© 1995 Senn-Delaney Leadership Consulting Group, Inc.

Figure 8.7

The High-Performance Culture Pyramid provides a visual representation of the building blocks of a culture that work together effectively, creating value for customers and consistently moving toward the vision that ignites the organization. However, this culture does not guarantee success in the marketplace. Even the best companies get out of sync with the market, develop layers of bureaucratic fat, or mend together solutions to today's problems which solidify over time into bureaucratic procedures and processes. Every company needs

to rethink itself periodically and apply the "clean sheet" principles of reengineering to its processes. The high-performance
culture provides a firm foundation for those efforts.

A Process to Discover and Develop Your Own High-Performance Culture

Over the past decades we have developed several processes
that work well in assisting a group of leaders to identify their
vision and high-performance values. These proven processes
are based on our discovery that vision and values need to come
from the heart and not the head. This usually requires having
the senior team go to a relaxing off-site location with few business agendas. There, teambuilding activities and open-ended
dialogue allow them to experience new values and new ways
of relating and communicating with each other. By having an
experience of an open, trusting environment, team interaction,
and supportive coaching and feedback, they can connect at an
emotional, not just intellectual level, with the kind of culture
they want for their organization and themselves.

This kind of setting is most conducive to identifying the
vision and values that touch and move people. Visions and
values cannot be developed through a logical, analytical process alone. When people connect to values very personally
they are also more willing to commit to living them.

Common Errors in Defining Corporate Culture

One of the most common errors in defining shared values is
that it often degenerates into a highly intellectual and imper-
sonal exercise or series of discussions. Values must come from
the heart and soul, not just the head or a flip chart.

A second error that organizations make in writing statements
of values and guiding behaviors is doing it in a **paternalistic**
way. Guiding behaviors should be written so that each and
every employee in the organization can own them. Statements
like, "we will develop our people" perpetuates dependence and
hierarchy. A more appropriate statement is, "we are committed
to continuous personal and professional growth."

9

~~~~~~~~~~~~~~~~~~~~

PHASE V: SUCCESSFUL IMPLEMENTATION OF CULTURE CHANGE

Successfully integrating new business processes into a corporation is no small feat. In fact, most reengineering failures are really failures in implementation. A concurrent culture change process is synergistic with reengineering and will improve the chances for successful implementation of newly reengineered systems and processes.

This synergy works because the successful implementation of reengineering requires a shift from a functional (vertical) orientation to a process (horizontal) orientation, where people in the organization must now focus on common objectives across traditional departmental boundaries. The practical problem with the implementation of such a shift is that to be successful, employees must know each other, trust each other, and learn to openly communicate with those in other departments. In many traditional, vertically structured organizations, such cross-departmental cooperation and communication has not been the case, and in many cultures, it was not encouraged either. Thus, a culture of mistrust and weak horizontal communications is heavily ingrained with informal systems and strong behavioral norms that hinder reengineering.

A culture change process brings about just such broad, cross-functional interactions, especially when culture change training and cross-functional teambuilding are combined with changes in the daily business behaviors and reinforced through company-wide communications and people actively coaching one another. Culture Change is a necessary platform for reengineering success.

THE POWER OF BELIEFS

In order to implement a successful culture change, it's useful to understand what cultural habits look like and how they develop in organizations and in people.

Cultural habits can be vividly seen in the interactive exercises that take place in our Executive Leadership and Culture Change seminars. In one such activity, we put people in pairs and ask them to score points. In most cases they automatically assume that their job is to beat the other person and score more points. If we have multiple pairs in the room, each pair will assume that they have to beat the other pairs. If we divide them into two groups, one group will assume that they have to beat the second group. In most all these cases, beating the other person was not a part of the instructions and not in fact how the game is won, yet nearly everyone assumes that's the objective.

What's the root of this strong habit in individuals and in groups? Most of us have grown up since childhood taking part in games where there was a winner and a loser. That strong habit, combined with the high internal drive for results of most business executives leads to the belief that **"for me to win, someone else has to lose."** Over time, this belief becomes an unconscious habit that "colors" many activities in a person's business life, often at the expense of others within the company. We're convinced that more energy is spent on internal competition in some organizations than meeting competitive threats from the outside.

In the "score points" example we just gave, people see the objective of the exercise through their own filters, including the belief "that for me to win, someone has to lose." Since beliefs largely determine behaviors, and behaviors determine results, the individuals and teams act dysfunctionally.

The influence of beliefs on behaviors and results is illustrated below.

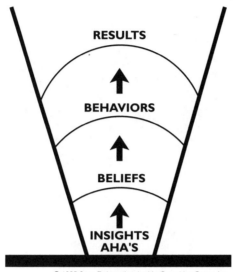

© 1995 Senn-Delaney Leadership Consulting Group, Inc.

Our beliefs influence our behaviors and they in turn determine our results.

A second phenomenon which influences our behaviors can be illustrated by the figure below. What is your immediate impression of what it is?

And what do you see at first glance in the figure below?

If you saw a rabbit in the first figure, you may have missed the duck that is also there. Or vice versa. The same holds true in the figure that has both angels and bats (or devils). The two phenomenon illustrated are Selective Perception and Lock-in/ Lock-out. In life we tend to only see a small portion of what is in front of us, only a few of the many personality traits of other people, only one way to view a situation, one way to look at decisions, and only a few ingredients in culture. The problem is that once we see something in a given way, we tend to lock-in and believe that it is the only way, or "the truth."

This all comes together in the "score points" exercise described earlier where people locked-in to a win-lose belief, and then saw everything through that fixed belief. Many of the limiting beliefs we encounter in organizations can be translated into cultural barriers.

Some of the most common beliefs are shown below:

LIMITING BELIEFS		
Belief	⇌	*Behavior*
It's safest to do what you are told	⇌	Lack of initiative
You can't admit mistakes around here	⇌	Blaming & excuses for lack of results
To do a job well, you have to do it by yourself	⇌	Poor delegation
That's not my job	⇌	Narrow focus
The legal department's only job is to avoid any risk	⇌	Stonewalls ideas, no attempt at creative solutions
If I appreciate an employee who's not perfect, they'll slack off & not improve	⇌	No appreciative feedback, lower morale
If I give someone constructive feedback they'll think I don't like them	⇌	Lack of development and coaching
There's more pain for failing than there is reward for succeeding	⇌	Safe, non-risk behaviors
Finance and Controls' job is to police expenses	⇌	Restrictive controls and lack of useful decision tools

IMPLEMENTING CULTURE CHANGE

In order to change behaviors and reshape a culture, a process is needed to unfreeze these locked-in beliefs and habitual behaviors. The process of unfreezing organizational beliefs is very different from those which are used for the development of organizational structure or a strategic plan. Changing mind-set requires a different learning methodology and process, one that is often less familiar and therefore initially somewhat less comfortable for organizations in need of change.

This creates another culture change rule not stated earlier, and that is,

A CULTURE WILL TEND TO REJECT AND RESIST WHAT IT
MOST NEEDS TO HELP CHANGE IT

For example, cultures that are very rational and analytical will only want to use rational and analytical processes to change the culture. Since human behaviors and beliefs are not rational and logical, that's a recipe for failure.

The successful implementation of a change in corporate culture requires a series of specially designed non-traditional interventions. Research into behavior change has shown that there are two primary ways to modify behavior. One is traditional "behavior modification" through reinforcement activities such as rewards and performance appraisals. While reinforcement is one element of culture change, it by itself is not powerful enough to shift an entrenched culture. Behavior modification including performance appraisal is far too slow in changing behaviors, it is often too indirect and tends to be externally, not internally, driven.

Research has shown that people develop a powerful internal drive to change only when they have an emotionally powerful "transformational experience." You probably know of at least one business executive who has either had a heart attack or bypass surgery, and the experience was so profound that they wound up changing their ways. The workaholic, cheeseburger-eating person you once knew is now a dedicated runner and somewhat of an evangelist about fat-free foods! Life changed due to a "transformational" experience. Similar changes are seen following a divorce, the death of a loved one, or the birth of a child. Emotional experience often causes one to step back from their old life patterns, reexamine their beliefs and behaviors, become committed to rebuilding a life with more balance and meaning than before. The significant emotional event creates an "unfreezing" and "openness for change" that didn't exist before, even though the dangers of lack of exercise, poor eating habits, poor communications at home, etc. are all well known.

Similarly, to shift corporate culture, the employees of the organization must have a significant transformational experience that causes them to develop an openness for change that didn't exist before. While this experience can come from such business events as a near bankruptcy, takeover attempt, precipitous drop in sales or income, fear of job loss, or a competitive attack on their core business, these events are external and often create a reactive, fear-driven response. A positive proactive transformational experience can be created through the implementation of specially designed "culture change" seminars for managers and employees. Once employees truly "feel" the need for change and experience how much better their business (and personal) life can be in a new, high-performance culture, there is a quantum leap in commitment to the change process.

To be most effective in shifting culture, the transformational experience must focus on the Values and Guiding Behaviors that define the desired new culture. By focusing on a new set of business values and daily behaviors that spell out "success" in the new culture, employees have an opportunity in the seminar to "live" the new culture, to practice the new behaviors, discuss the new values and how they apply to work, and gain a comfort and familiarity with the changes being asked of them.

Since it turns out that the values and the behaviors for corporate excellence are also principles of personal life effectiveness, people end up working to change themselves "for themselves," and not just for the company. This makes the change even more appealing and more internally driven.

Once an openness to change has been developed, the old ways of doing things need to be replaced with a set of new business behaviors. If employees gain a readiness for change during the culture change seminars, but come back into the same old work environment, with the same old rules, policies, procedures, and supervisory behaviors, it is easy to go back to their old ways, and the openness for change is quickly extinguished. Like the person home from bypass surgery, to effectively change their lives, they need to change their daily routine. They must clean out the refrigerator of unhealthy foods, set up an exercise schedule, revise their work hours, etc.

In a similar way, the company must change daily business behaviors. These most frequently reside in the policies, systems, and procedures that govern the daily activities of employees.

Many of the most powerful policies and procedures lie in the area of Human Resources. For example, to change work behaviors, people need to be evaluated and promoted differently, in accordance with the new cultural values, not the old rules. There are a number of HR systems, including hiring, employee orientation, performance reviews, compensation mechanisms, and others that need to be shifted to be in alignment with the new cultural values. By shifting systems and procedures, employees begin doing things differently, and the change will gain depth and a sense of permanency.

Another important part of reinforcement, is the organization's communications process. An active communication process should be established, with newsletters and articles devoted to depicting those employees who are "living" the new values. In addition, the development of a feedback-rich environment is critical. In such an environment individuals are actively encouraged to coach each other, give both appreciative and constructive feedback, and measure themselves and their work teams against the new values and guiding behaviors.

Culture Change =

Transformation + Behavioral Change + Reinforcement
"Unfreezing"   "Shift"   "Refreezing"

Three of the most high impact elements in the successful implementation of culture change are:

- Transformational Training (the "Unfreezing" piece);
- Revised Human Resource Systems (the Behavior "Shift" piece); and
- Corporate Communications (the overall Reinforcement and "Refreezing" piece).

Transformational Training

Over the past several decades, Training has often become synonymous with "nice to do, when we get some extra time or money!" To many senior business executives, training is usually thought of as "motivation," "lecturing," "technical skills development," or "touchy-feely people stuff," and certainly not seen with the same degree of importance as the "hard skills" of strategic planning, product design, financial analysis, or reengineering. While companies will spend millions on strategic planning engagements or reengineering, they balk at spending significant dollars on managerial and employee non-technical training.

In our experience, training is not a "nice to do," but a "must do" for reengineering success, as well as the only way to successfully shift corporate culture. An analysis of typical reengineering projects shows that less than 10% of the reengineering budget is usually set aside for training (Source: *Reengineering: The Critical Success Factors*). We believe this figure is low, especially considering the rather dismal report card for reengineering success.

According to a recent interview (Wall Street Journal articles, Jan. 2 & 24, 1995), Michael Hammer and James Champy have also come to the conclusion that training is a key ingredient in reengineering success:

> **Hammer:** *"If you're serious about treating people as an asset, we're looking at a dramatic increase in the investment in them. I tell companies they need to quintuple their investment in education..."*

> **Champy:** *"You also have to teach more behavioral things. Now that we've given you more control, how do you behave and make decisions—from how do you deal with a worker who isn't functioning, to what do you do when a customer asks for something that isn't in the rule book."*

Our research and experience confirms that just $600–$800 additional dollars of the right kind of training per employee can best help ensure culture change and significantly improve the odds of reengineering success.

Specialized "Culture Change" trainings are an effective and efficient method of shifting corporate culture. Properly conceived and delivered, these seminars and workshops not only create a shift in the culture, but also prepare an openness for change that allows the reengineering process to take hold and develop.

Traditional lecture or motivational type seminars are not effective in shifting corporate culture. While the information may be excellent, culture-shift is not just about new ideas or information as much as it is about creating personal change in the employees who comprise the culture. Research has found that individuals learn best that which they "experience," as opposed to that which they just hear or read about. In the case of culture change, an old saying aptly applies:

*I hear, I understand; I do, I learn; I **experience**, I **change**!*

The most effective "transformational" training technology for culture change is what we call "insight-based learning." It produces "aha's" which cause people to reexamine previously held beliefs and habitual behaviors. It does so through structured experiences combined with reflective time which promotes deeper personal and organizational learning.

Training based on the techniques of "insight learning" can best be described as a highly interactive process whereby participants take active accountability for their own learning and interact with the material, the facilitators, and the other seminar participants through a series of active discussions, team exercises, personal introspection, group dynamics, business evaluations, and open sharing of ideas and feelings. This more holistic approach allows the seminar participants to integrate the knowledge from the seminar with their own personal experiences. That shifts old habitual ways of thinking and interacting to new, more appropriate and effective ideas and behaviors. It is only through personal change in attitudes and behavior that an old culture can be "unfrozen" and an openness for culture change developed.

Transformational training is most effective when it is customized and developed for the needs, culture, and style of the organization involved. In most cases, the customization is based on the findings from the initial culture audit, as well as the issues and discussions that surface during the Senior Management Off-site Retreat that takes place early in the culture change process. In addition, to produce lasting results, culture change training must be designed to integrate business issues into the personal transformation process. In that way, the transformational experience of the participants is put into immediate use to help solve the immediate business needs of the organization.

One of the key means of integrating business issues into the culture change and personal transformational process is to begin the culture change seminar with the basic questions that seem to be on people's minds during times of change:

Why do we need to change?
From what to what?
How are we going to get there?
What does this mean to me?

We have come to call this initial seminar module: "The Business Challenge." By developing an experiential learning module which interactively helps the participants answer for themselves these key questions, seminar participants quickly begin to see the applicability of the culture change skills they are learning in the seminar to their "real world" of work. We find that a multimedia approach tends to work best, with a short custom video on change, an outside speaker, perhaps even an actual company financial "scenario" where the only real solution is a change in culture and the fundamental redesign of the business. By opening each seminar with the "Business Challenge" (sometimes called the "Business Opportunity," or even, "Our Business Problem"), the participants quickly experience personal insight and value, the session takes on a whole new form of relevancy for their own personal lives and there is more "buy-in" or "ownership" in the change process.

To be effective, change seminars need to reach a "critical mass" of employees before real change can take hold. While culture change must start at the top, just having the senior team experience the change workshop is not sufficient for a shift in culture. One of our early lessons as change management consultants was that if you want to change your behavior, surround yourself with those who are of like mind and who are willing to coach and remind you. As one of the authors found while training for his first marathon, the support, encouragement, and coaching of a group of friends was essential to develop the new exercise habits it takes to adequately train for a 26.2 mile race!

Our consulting and change management experience tells us that a critical mass of approximately 40–60% of employees is necessary before the culture-shift process begins to develop a life and momentum of its own. As more and more people experience the new culture, practice the new skills and behaviors, see the benefits in the new cultural values, and begin to clearly see a new vision of how things could work, the change process begins to gather momentum.

Another highly effective design element in the entire process of culture change involves a "cascading approach" to the culture change seminars. This starts after the senior session when individual members of the senior team lead their own departmental teams through the culture change seminar. In this way, a participant in the senior session now becomes the leader of their own team session, and must become doubly accountable for not only living the new cultural values, but also supporting the overall culture change process.

We have also found that by conducting the seminars within a "natural" work group, it is possible to gain peer support and reinforcement and to more easily focus on issues where the newly learned behaviors and change management skills can be used to solve current business problems.

Experience has shown that a broad-based culture change process is most effective when it is seen as an important company event, and least effective when it is seen as another "training program." One has high visibility and relevancy, the other is seen by employees as mere "compliance" or simply "training" without any immediate or obvious application to the real world of work. To signal that the culture change process is "important to the business," it is recommended that it be linked to a significant business improvement process, like Total Quality, Reengineering or Restructuring.

REVISING HUMAN RESOURCE SYSTEMS

"If you want to get people's attention, fiddle with their pay check."

—Anonymous

As a result of new insights gained during the culture change seminars, organizations and work teams tend to define and commit to new behaviors. Unfortunately without ongoing reinforcement it's difficult to permanently change culture. The most effective reinforcement systems reside in Human Resources. Too often, training programs alone are expected to permanently change behavior. Unless the HR systems, policies and procedures are altered to be in alignment with the new cultural values, old behaviors will tend to dominate.

While reengineering requires a shift from Functional to Process-Orientation, it follows that to be in alignment, compensation and other reward and recognition systems must shift from the traditional individual-focus, to a new focus on team and overall organizational performance. The entire compensation program should be reviewed, including salary, bonus and incentive plans, and job descriptions.

In addition, new hiring profiles should be developed to assist managers in making appropriate selection decisions. Since managers tend to hire in their own image, carefully detailed profiles will enable them to recognize the necessary skills needed in today's business environment and the values and attitudes that match the new culture.

Another key system change that has a great deal of impact on culture and employee behaviors is goal setting, and particularly, the budgeting process. John Davis, CFO for Riggs National Bank of Washington DC attended a senior management culture change seminar along with the other senior officers of Riggs right in the middle of the annual budget process. Prior to the shared experience off-site, Davis and others were complaining about the difficulty of getting people to cooperate and share resources in arriving at the rolled up budget figures.

"Everybody was out to protect their own department and no one was willing to give up resources, people, or most importantly, dollars to support another area of the bank. I've been through dozens of these kinds of 'wars' and it gets really tiring. We finally arrive at a good budget, but the conflict and gamesmanship gets old!"

Following the culture change seminar, Davis and the senior team finished the budget easily, not because they talked about it during the off-site, but because they all agreed to a new set of team behaviors where the main focus was what's good for the corporation and not just one individual department. A new set of behaviors—specifically support and trust—were practiced during the seminar and quickly became the new norm at the top of the organization.

Perhaps the strongest of all internal business systems is "who gets promoted and why?" In many ways the culture is defined and the rules for success are contained in the written, and more importantly, unwritten, promotion policies and examples. In the past, many promotions occurred because of loyalty and tenure.

To break old cultural habits, the Columbia Gas Reengineering Teams were formed by purposely seeking out "change agents" at all levels of the organization for the team, not just certain "levels" or "pay grades." It quickly became obvious that the new culture being developed was going to be more performance-driven than the old culture. For example, Reengineering Core Team members from middle management were given the opportunity to take positions of leadership within the team and make presentations to senior management, where their excellent analytical and leadership skills became recognized. As a result of the visibility of the various members of the Reengineering Team and their activities across functional lines in redesigning the organization, a parallel effort to redesign job descriptions and promotional policies was undertaken, further bringing the policies and procedures in alignment with the new culture. These new job descriptions and requirements for promotion focus more heavily than before on specific skills, attitudes, and leadership behaviors.

Additional Reinforcements: Communications and Cultural Symbols

Culture also resides in words, stories and symbols. Reshaping a culture requires new language, symbols and words. Since culture change is largely an emotional process, specially developed communications and symbolic reinforcement are needed to reinforce and perpetuate the new culture. Such activities become a tangible vehicle of the transformation and are extremely powerful.

Some of the most effective communications and feedback activities stem directly from the culture change seminars themselves. For example, in our customized culture change seminars for clients we routinely assist each participant in developing a Personal Commitment and are able to convert that to a handy pocket card, that can be carried at all times. These Personal Contracts are statements of behavioral change that the individual commits to implement. It is not uncommon for a CEO or a middle manager to be talking to a group of employees about the need for culture change, pull out their personal contract and share it with the employees as an indication that everyone needs to change.

Following each culture change workshop, it is appropriate for the group to get back together again to discuss what they have learned, how they plan on implementing the culture change activities, and how they can best support one another in fulfilling their personal commitments. Sometimes the group creates its own set of posters and reminders, plastering the walls with reinforcement messages. Often someone will have the idea to put a few reinforcement slogans on the network screen-saver, so it shows up on all computers daily. Even e–mail messages about the importance of change and the new culture begin to show up on electronic bulletin boards. Often special note pads are printed up with slogans reminding everyone about the new cultural values.

If you want a live example of building the new culture into the work environment, visit the Administration and Corporate Services areas of Bell Atlantic at their offices in Arlington, Virginia. Several floors are "plastered" with signs, slogans, charts, banners, Blue Chips, and other tangible evidence of The Bell Atlantic Way culture and behaviors. For example, as you walk through the cubicles and down corridors, "street signs" with such names as "Accountability Avenue," "Be Here Now Place," "Coaching Boulevard" and "Feedback Lane" guide employees through their work day. It is easy to feel the energy and spirit of The Bell Atlantic Way behaviors as you enter the floor. At a chance meeting in the Men's Room on one of the floors, one of the authors decided to test the reality of the culture. Standing next to an employee at the wash basin, he asked: "All those signs are pretty neat gimmicks." To which the person replied: "They aren't just signs; it's a way-of-life around here. The Bell Atlantic Way behaviors are critical to our competitive success!"

Other appropriate communication activities include video presentations depicting the values and behaviors of the new culture. Monthly "dialogue" days can be set aside for informal meetings on the new values. Newsletters and other publications can feature articles on "cultural heroes," and employees should be recognized and rewarded for their efforts wherever possible. Signs and posters can also be used strategically to further communicate the business mission. Clubs and athletic teams are additional vehicles for building and promoting team spirit.

10

PHASE VI: MEASUREMENT AND ONGOING IMPROVEMENT

The actions of men are the best interpreters of their thoughts.

—John Locke

What gets measured gets people's attention!

—Anonymous

Like nothing else before, reengineering is responsible for legitimizing a whole new range of non-financial measurements useful in successfully managing today's complex businesses. Once thought of as "soft" issues, measures of Customer Satisfaction, Best Practices, Process Cycle Time, Design Cycle Time, and Corporate Culture are becoming important indices. However, it is not easy to measure these less tangible elements, particularly on the behavioral side.

For years, companies have been attempting to measure the attitude of employees (and by inference the overall corporation) through the use of attitude and opinion surveys. While these have been somewhat useful in recording how people feel about such issues as benefits, supervision, management, service levels, quality, etc., as a whole they have been ineffective in providing insight into how to improve employee and overall corporate performance. One of the failings of these "attitude" surveys is that they often depend upon the "feeling" at the moment, and thus are subject to the normal ups and downs of human personality and quarterly performance.

The results of opinion surveys can change with the announcement of a restructuring or during a difficult labor negotiation. What is really being measured is how people "feel" about things, not how individuals and teams are functioning. While feelings are useful in gauging performance, they do not really give us insight into the root causes of performance shortfalls or customer problems.

We believe that attitude surveys are in some way a part of the older business paradigm. They are in part a hold over from the "unwritten contract" that companies had with employees:

> *"We'll take care of you and provide for your security, and you give us your dedication and loyalty."*

Since high-performance behaviors and high-performance teams create results for organizations (and fulfillment for individuals), it is more important to ask about levels of cross-organizational teamwork than about how people feel. It is more important to know that there is a bias for action and a can-do attitude, than there is to know if people are unhappy about declining medical benefits.

We believe a whole new approach to measuring and monitoring organizational and individual performance is needed to provide today's corporations with a more effective set of performance improvement tools. Instead of seeking to measure attitudes, we suggest measuring "behaviors" of actual performance-related activities. When it comes to measuring culture change, what better behaviors or actions to evaluate than the Guiding Behaviors that constitute the newly desired corporate culture?

In addition, performance measures are more effective and contain more useful information if they come from different sources. Imagine the analogy of a sailor, out in the open ocean, trying to determine his exact position. Basing current position on the last sighting would be disaster, and dead-reckoning equally erroneous. Experienced sailors rely on several different inputs or sightings to effectively determine position. Accurately determining corporate culture, individual effectiveness, or other organizational measurements similarly requires multiple inputs.

CULTURAL METRICS: ESTABLISHING BASELINE MEASUREMENTS

The Corporate Culture Profile, discussed in Chapter 6 is a "macro" look at the culture taken prior to the culture change. Once the culture has been defined with Shared Core Values and Guiding Behaviors, it is important to more accurately measure the organization and individuals against those definitions.

An effective individual measure is a "360° Feedback Inventory," which we typically call the Living the Values 360° Feedback Inventory[SM]. A similar measurement instrument for the entire organization is called the Organizational Guiding Behaviors Inventory[SM].

• ORGANIZATIONAL GUIDING BEHAVIORS INVENTORY[SM]

It is relatively easy to build an Organizational Guiding Behaviors Inventory[SM]. For each of the Shared Core Values, a list of six to ten specific Guiding Behaviors can be developed. All employees then fill out an Organizational Guiding Behaviors questionnaire, rating the degree to which the company is currently displaying these important behaviors during the daily performance of work.

The Organizational Guiding Behaviors Inventory is a "snapshot" of the culture as it currently exists, measured in terms of the elements in the "desired" culture. While it is impossible to "see" culture, or even values, they tend to come to life in these day-to-day actions and behaviors of employees, and are effectively measured.

Figure 10.1 shows an example of the summary "overview" data from a sample Organizational Guiding Behaviors Inventory. The overview lists the composite score for a Core Value category on a scale of one to five. The scores for each Value are the average of all the scores for the six to ten Guiding Behaviors that define that Core Value. As you can see, this organization is currently strong in Leadership, Integrity and Winning, which indicates a very performance-driven company. At the same time, the company seems weakest in Feedback and Coaching.

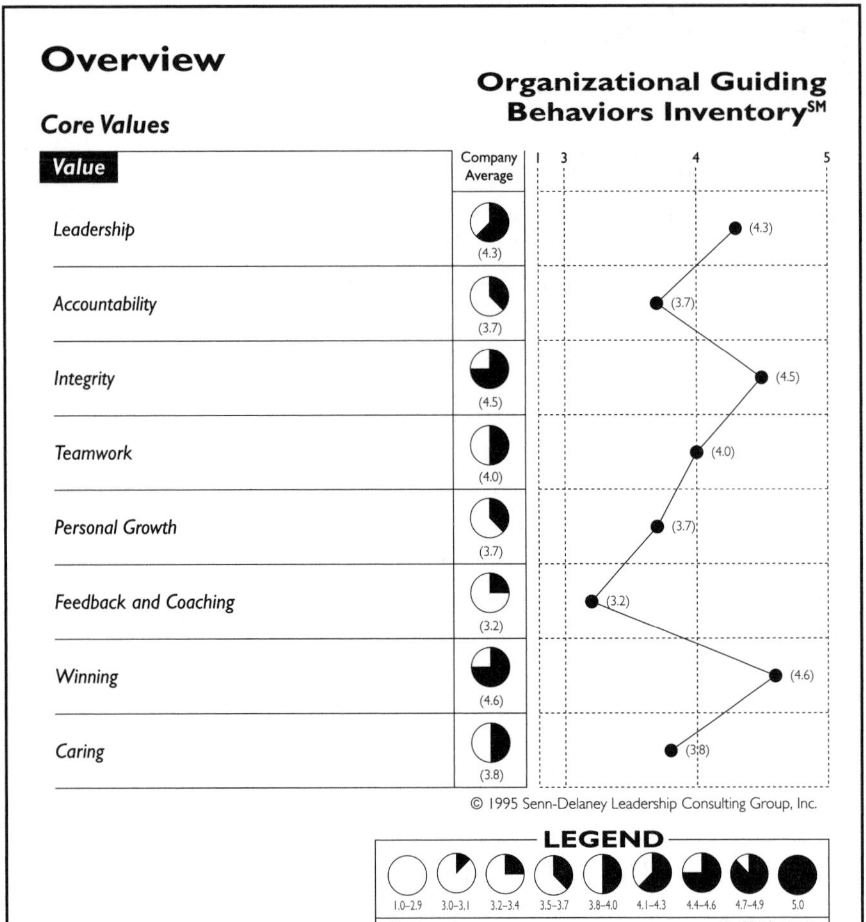

Figure 10.1

Figure 10.2 shows one individual Value, in this case, Teamwork, and the scores for each of the Guiding Behaviors. While the overall average is 4.0, most of the low marks come from people focusing on a win for their area or department, and not contributing to broader wins for the organization. Such daily behavior is particularly damaging when an organization is trying to implement reengineering. As this figure also shows, improvement is needed in the organization on resolving conflict between departments, again indicating that teamwork is strong within, but not across departments.

Teamwork Value

Organizational Guiding Behaviors Inventory^{SM}

Guiding Behaviors	Average Scores as seen by...						Total Company
	Senior Management	Finance & Admin.	Manufacturing	Sales / Marketing	Engineering	Information Systems	AVERAGE
1) People tend to act for the long-term benefit of the total company, even if it may take away from short-term benefits.	(3.5)	(3.1)	(2.5)	(3.0)	(2.9)	(3.0)	(3.0)
2) People support their teammates so the whole team can accomplish the objective.	(5.0)	(4.8)	(4.6)	(4.9)	(4.5)	(4.9)	(4.8)
3) This company promotes teamwork through recognition and rewards.	(4.0)	(3.7)	(2.9)	(4.1)	(3.2)	(3.7)	(3.6)
4) We are encouraged to resolve conflicts with other areas of the company.	(4.0)	(2.0)	(2.8)	(3.1)	(2.9)	(2.6)	(2.9)
5) Team training is a regularly used technique in this company and is supported by management.	(3.8)	(4.0)	(3.6)	(4.5)	(4.2)	(3.9)	(4.0)
6) New employees are quickly brought into the team.	(4.8)	(4.9)	(5.0)	(5.0)	(4.7)	(4.8)	(4.8)
7) Cross-functional teams are often used to solve problems.	(4.4)	(4.4)	(3.9)	(4.0)	(4.4)	(4.6)	(4.3)
8) Supervisor and department head regularly hold team meetings where everyone is encouraged to speak up.	(4.5)	(4.7)	(4.0)	(4.3)	(4.7)	(4.8)	(4.5)
Average	(4.3)	(3.9)	(3.7)	(4.1)	(3.9)	(4.0)	(4.0)

© 1995 Senn-Delaney Leadership Consulting Group, Inc.

LEGEND

1.0-2.9	3.0-3.1	3.2-3.4	3.5-3.7	3.8-4.0	4.1-4.3	4.4-4.6	4.7-4.9	5.0

1.0 = Never ← → 5.0 = Consistently

Figure 10.2

It is important to develop an Organizational Guiding Behaviors Inventory early on in the process of reengineering and culture change, as this can serve as a baseline measure for the new culture being developed. Once this baseline is established, it will tell the entire organization where they are currently displaying the new cultural values and behaviors, and where the new values and behaviors need greater attention and improvement. By measuring behaviors and activities, not attitudes or feelings, a more accurate representation of the current corporate culture is developed. Using this baseline and performing a simple "gap analysis," allows everyone to see where the current culture is strong and where it is weak.

VALUE OF ESTABLISHING A BASELINE MEASURE OF CULTURE

- Provide a measurement of the organization's behaviors relative to the Shared Values and Guiding Behaviors.

- Provide feedback on how well the organization is making the new culture a reality in day-to-day activities.

- Send a clear message to the entire organization that living the new culture is important.

- Enable the leaders to measure and pay attention to Guiding Behaviors, which are the greatest levers in sustaining change.

- The data can be used to develop action plans for personal and organizational improvement.

As with any process of change, and particularly for reengineering and culture change, the Organizational Guiding Behaviors Inventory is more than just an event, it's a way of life for that new culture. This cultural "reading" should be taken at least once a year, and during intense times of culture-shaping or change activities, twice a year is appropriate.

Once an Organizational Guiding Behaviors Inventory has been completed, we recommend communicating the results to the entire corporation. This will let all employees know how they are living the new culture and what areas need everyone's attention and accountability for improvement. Training programs, discussion groups, and Action Teams can be formed to focus on those areas of behaviors showing the biggest gaps. With each successive "reading," an organization which is truly committed will steadily grow stronger and stronger as it works to make the new culture a daily way of life.

- "LIVING THE VALUES" 360° FEEDBACK INVENTORY[SM]

> *"O wad some power the giftie gie us to see oursel's as others see us."*

—Robert Burns

In these times of rapid change, individuals as well as organizations need to take stock and reinvent themselves. Unfortunately, the majority of managers do not understand their specific strengths and weaknesses very well. We all tend to see ourselves in favorable "light." Recent data shows that only about 1/3 of managers produce self-assessments that match what their co-workers concluded about them.

Even though there is great value in being able see how we come across to others, most people get very little useful feedback on the job. For some, there is no formal feedback, for others, there may be some feedback once a year through the eyes of one person, that is, the boss.

For all these reasons, more and more companies have begun to use a 360° Feedback Inventory which gathers input anonymously from peers, direct reports, direct supervision, and in some cases, the customer or client.

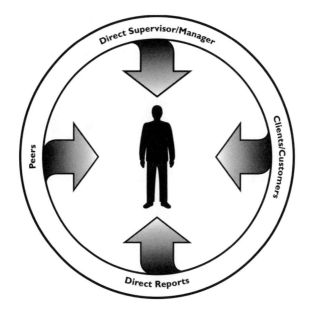

A 360° Feedback Inventory is an exceptional tool for personal development and to "see" how someone is living the values and guiding behaviors of the new culture. By getting confidential feedback from all directions (peers, direct reports, customers, and immediate manager) an individual can effectively see the "shadow" they cast in terms of role modeling the corporate culture. Individuals can instantly create greater awareness of themselves and their impact on others through this "360° feedback" process. They will also better understand those areas where they are doing well. A sample profile is shown in Figure 10.3.

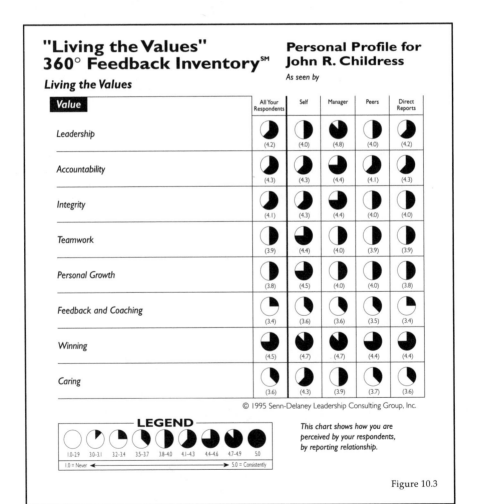

Figure 10.3

The Individual 360° is a benchmark reading for each individual so that with each successive 360° survey, individuals will be able to see where growth appeared and what areas are still needing improvement. (See Figure 10.4.)

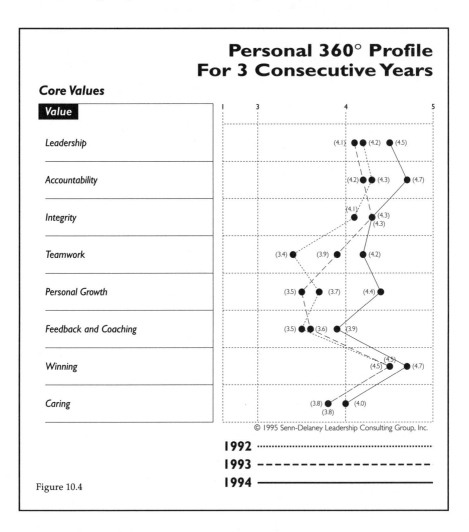

Figure 10.4

While the 360° Feedback Inventory process has been found to be very valuable, its role is best seen as a supplement rather than a replacement for the Employee Review process. Anonymous feedback has been found to be more objective when used in a supporting role rather than the primary role in an employee evaluation. The reason is probably because those giving the feedback are more likely to be direct and honest if they know it is not the only input that counts for someone's promotion or lack of it.

A number of leading companies that have made significant progress in changing their corporate culture by extending the 360° process to the training area as well. Behind each characteristic an employee is evaluated on, one or more training programs may be developed that can support an individual to improve their skills and behaviors.

BENEFITS OF 360° FEEDBACK INVENTORY

- A useful snapshot of how the individual is seen as "living" the organization's values and guiding behaviors.

- A non-threatening and confidential mechanism for team members and associates to give each other developmental feedback.

- A useful road map for improvement.

- Increased awareness of your leadership abilities and team behavior through precise feedback from your manager, peers, direct reports and customers.

- A vehicle for effective coaching.

360° DOS AND DON'TS

If we truly want to reengineer a culture, we also need to "reengineer" the individuals within that culture. Unfortunately the 360° is usually not developed, utilized or administered in a way which best promotes the desired culture change. If the 360° is to be a powerful tool in culture change—and it can be—then the following common errors need to be avoided.

- *Don't… use a generic or "off-the-shelf" 360°*

The majority of companies use standard or generic 360°s. We believe these are ineffective in shaping a culture. If the culture has been defined in terms of a set of behaviors (A, B, C) and the 360° measures a different set of behaviors (D, E, F), the feedback is not nearly as useful.

For that reason, the 360° should be totally customized based upon the organization's own defined values and guiding behaviors. If teamwork has been defined by five guiding behavior statements, then those same five statements should be used to define teamwork in the 360°. In that way the 360° can be an exceptional tool to enable the individual to "see" how they're living the values and guiding behaviors of the new culture.

The initial 360° can become a benchmark for each individual so that with each successive 360° survey, individuals will be able to see where growth appeared and what areas are still needing improvement.

- *Do…start the 360° process with Senior Management*

Based on principles of culture change, the 360° Inventory should be developed and used first by the senior team, including the CEO. It is this group that casts the farthest "shadow" and if they are not effectively role modeling the elements and behaviors of the new culture, the organization won't, no matter how much training or support is given.

When the senior team completes their 360° Feedback Inventory and openly discusses it with their subordinates, much is accomplished. It is a sign of added openness and trust in the culture, and it increases the readiness of the next levels to take part in the 360° themselves.

- *Don't…introduce the 360° in ways which are threatening to people*

All too often the way in which the 360° is introduced creates anxiety, especially if employees think their jobs may be at stake because of this one measurement. The 360° can be a very positive individual development tool, when administered correctly.

People rely on "measurement" in many day-to-day activities. Look at activities such as dieting, family budgeting, golf scoring, sports "ladder" standings, health measures, and exercise schedules. We, as critical-thinking human beings have always and will always "score" ourselves to see how we are doing from one day to another, in almost any walk of life. Who doesn't have a weight scale in their house?

As long as the results from these measurements are kept "private" (i.e., how many people know how much you weigh?) and shared at the discretion of the owner of these results, most people view these measures as informative and productive. Once the private nature of these measures are made public, the individual is susceptible to comparisons and negative remarks. The measures go from personally motivating to somewhat intimidating.

Likewise, individual 360° Behavior scores at work should initially be "confidential." As the organization as a whole begins to embrace change and value personal development, more and more individuals will share their performance measures with others in order to benefit from coaching and positive suggestions.

We find that the 360° is readily embraced when utilized in the following format:

- It corresponds with the defined definition of culture.

- It is administered after people have personal exposure to the cultural values in a culture change seminar.

- Confidentiality is ensured by giving them a great deal of control over the instrument, by being able to hand it out themselves and receive back the results without others in the company having access to it.

- The 360° process begins with the senior team and then moves down in the organization.

Putting Teeth in Culture Change

If an organization embarks upon a serious culture change initiative, defines culture, coaches people on behaviors and then tolerates senior leaders who visibly violate the culture, they jeopardize the entire change initiative.

One CEO not long ago told us that several managers had come to him recently to talk about one of their peers, the president of a major division and a direct report to the CEO. They believed the entire culture change initiative was in jeopardy because after continual coaching and discussion, this individual continued to behave counter to the newly stated culture, and in fact belittled the culture change initiative to employees. Their words to the CEO were, "many people feel that the culture change process will lose all credibility if this is the way a member of the senior team is allowed to behave!"

A shot was heard by leaders around the world when Jack Welch, General Electric's respected and pragmatic Chairman, announced that executives who did not live up to GE's values—even if they produced results—would not have a future in the company. As he told us in our interview:

> *"For years we looked the other way while executives drove an organization, intimidated our people and beat the results out of them to make the numbers. Today we do not believe this person will make it. We don't believe this behavior is sustainable. You need to live by our values, to energize every mind and get everybody involved to win in this globally competitive environment. You simply can't have that older leadership style."*

Jack Welch views values as so important that he defines the GE culture through their values, and finds ways to ensure that people live the values. Welch has introduced a model describing four types of leaders and how they are evaluated. It is designed to emphasize expected cultural behaviors. They are:

> *"The **Type 1 Leader** has the values and meets the numbers. That leader is brilliant. We would like a zillion of these. For them it is onward and upward.*

*"The **Type 2 Leader** is also easy—that is the leader who does not meet the commitment and does not share our values. While not as pleasant a call, it is just as easy to evaluate.*

*"Then you have the **Type 3 Leader,** who has the values and does not meet the numbers. That person gets a second chance. You have got to keep coaching and hoping. And we have some great success stories about this kind of leader changing, although nowhere near the amount we would like. It is well known that we do give people who live the values a second chance.*

*"The **Type 4 Leader** is one who meets the numbers but does not share the values we believe we must have. For years we looked the other way—today we do not believe the person will make it over a sustained period of time."*

Leadership Development Model

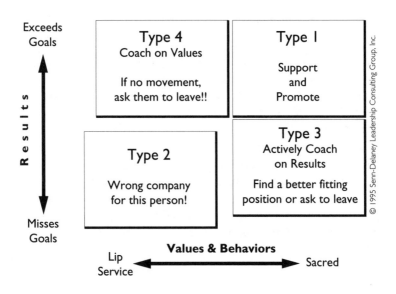

Once culture change begins to take on a life of its own, the organization needs to be willing to confront and visibly act on such issues in order to move the culture forward.

OTHER REINFORCEMENT TOOLS

When people are working on changing behaviors to support a new culture there are a variety of measurement tools that are useful. The most obvious one is the performance management or appraisal system. When explicit values and behaviors are made a part of the review, managers are forced to talk about behaviors with employees. The appraisal system can be made to carry more weight by tying compensation to the guiding behaviors. An energy services client tied a third of the potential performance bonus to a combination of living the Guiding Behaviors and efforts to implement the new culture. A large insurance client tied the new cultural values and guiding behaviors to the succession planning process. In fact the final decision to move the president into the CEO's role was in part dependent upon the Board and the retiring CEO's confidence that the new leader would effectively role model and perpetuate the newly emerging culture which was seen as a competitive advantage.

Other developmental tools can also be of assistance. In our own firm, we utilize a very simple and useful four quadrant matrix to assist people in learning about their own strengths and weaknesses, as well as helping them understand the importance of diversity and balance of life in order to maintain our own healthy culture.

Whatever measures or reinforcement tools an organization uses, the key ingredient is the spirit and commitment in which they are utilized by all involved. Reengineering is a major shock to an organization and well-intended measurement tools can guide and support an organization through these dramatic changes. It takes commitment by the leaders to present these measurements in the best way possible for the organization. Being committed to growing as leaders will only facilitate the openness to growth for the rest of the organization. These measurement tools are the important vehicles to drive reengineering through an organization.

11

OVERCOMING RESISTANCE TO CHANGE

Of all the problems and challenges faced in successfully implementing reengineering, overcoming resistance to change is probably the single greatest barrier. Resistance to change is natural. Leaders who truly understand the reasons behind the human experience of resistance to change can more effectively reduce that "natural" resistance and facilitate the change process. The primary reasons behind resistance to change are:

- Fear—Change means doing things differently and results in risk and the loss of a person's comfort zone. People's imaginations work overtime creating "fear of the imagined."

- Skepticism—Some change initiatives lack clear and obvious management commitment. No one wants to get geared up for a new way of working only to find out that management changed its mind or that it was just a passing fad.

- No perceived need—Why are we doing this? We're doing just fine. What's the need? What are the benefits?

As one middle manager said during a major change event in the organization:

All we want to know from senior management is two things:

- *Do you know what you're doing?*

- *Do you really care about us?*

How We Create Our Own Resistance

While it is true that there is a natural human phenomenon called "Resistance to Change," all too often the change process itself inadvertently heightens that resistance. The most common phenomenon we observe in reengineering efforts is as follows.

Outside consultants or inside change agents lead the study process assisted by people selected from various parts of the organization. This core reengineering team gets onboard and in some cases becomes almost evangelical about the changes, while the remaining organization only gets periodic glimpses of what is to come. Since the changes make so much sense to the team, they mistakenly believe that the ideas will be readily embraced by the operating organization. In reality there are dozens of modifications which need to be made to ultimately make the ideas work.

Because the reengineering team often lacks the behavioral skills and training needed to adequately sell new ideas, involve people, or understand resistance to change, they are ineffective in presenting the changes to the line managers who must implement them. The reengineering team then sees the organization as resistant and inflexible while the organization looks at the new ideas like "observer/critics" and is able to point out every possible flaw.

After studying some very successful leaders of process improvement, we have developed several hints to help executives more successfully lead the reengineering process. Basically the entire Change Management process revolves around two activities:

Stimulating enthusiasm and commitment, while at the same time minimizing the threat and fear involved with change.

While the following hints and suggestions have proven to be useful for numerous companies, like most other "tips," they really depend upon the attitude and state of mind of the people implementing them. At the core of all successful reengineering and culture change efforts is the fundamental point of view of service, caring and empathy.

If the leaders of the organization and the change process:

- see their mission as serving the customer and the well-being of the organization,
- demonstrate that they "really care" about people, and
- display empathy for those caught up in the fear,

then there is an excellent chance that they will find the right words at the right time, and find the right things to do that will allow people to transition smoothly through the change process. Employees will come out on the other side with healthy attitudes, accountability, and active involvement in creating the "new" organization.

ELIMINATION OF FEAR

Reengineering efforts cannot flourish in an environment of fear. And like any major change, reengineering brings forth a strong set of fears in all levels of employees:

What if I fail or am less competent in the new environment?
Will I be able to learn all the new stuff?
Will I still work with my friends?
Who will I report to?...is he/she fair?
Will I have to start all over?
What happens if I don't like the new environment?
Will there be layoffs? How will those laid off be treated?

Fear can create paralysis in an organization. We call it the "Bunker Mentality." This "heads down," "do only what I'm told" environment is the opposite of what is needed. Fear cannot be eliminated from the bottom-up. Leaders must establish an atmosphere where people are free to make suggestions and question decisions without fearing reprisal.

At Bell Atlantic, Brenda Morris worked to create a "fear-free" environment which she describes as follows:

"From the very beginning, we (the Reengineering Task Force) were a level-less environment. Anyone at any level could say or do anything with no risk. And believe me, they did. When they had something to say, they said it. There was no

retaliation for anything anyone said. They had lots of good ideas and they were able to share them with us. It forced us to step back and let go of some controlling behaviors... they were very good at giving us coaching.

"Once a week we would sit down and talk about The Bell Atlantic Way Behaviors and identify what we were doing well and what we weren't doing well. It gave us a framework for talking about how we wanted to work together. We probably spent about 25% of our time talking about the culture we wanted...how we would act towards each other and trust each other. It had to be an open forum...people couldn't hold back."

Eliminating fear also helps people be more receptive to feedback. At Bell Atlantic the reengineering team interviewed all the major customers and developed a set of customer requirements. The team rated themselves monthly on that set of requirements, asking themselves what they could do better, discovering root causes of errors or defects and developing ways to improve. They followed a similar evaluation process for internal customers. They also rated themselves on how well they were coaching others in the organization and making decisions and taking risks. They used these evaluations to determine training and additional resource needs.

SEEING THE INNOCENCE OF PEOPLE

It takes an aware and compassionate person to avoid judging those who are caught up in fear and resistance. The following may help improve your awareness and understanding. Imagine a time in your childhood when you went into a dark room and could not find the light switch. You may recall that your mind filled the room with monsters and "Bogeymen." Of course they weren't really there, but fear still surged through your body. Likewise, employees fear the unknown and darkness that is represented by reengineering and change. They are not necessarily trying to "tear the process down," they need some form of understanding and light to fill the darkness.

It takes a very savvy leader to see the numerous acts of resistance to change that go on in organizations as simply "acts of innocence." A leader who understands the nature of the human condition appreciates fully that the majority of people are not resisting out of some conscious motive, but rather they are simply "caught up in the grip of insecurity and negative thoughts" and their behavior is just that, innocent reactions out of insecurity and fear.

Too often, those in charge assume negative motives for the actions of employees during the stress and trials of the change process. And by ascribing "assumed motives" of revenge or willful resistance to the behavior of employees, they then take on a "defensive" attitude, which as everyone knows, just adds to the tension and difficulty of the communications process between human beings. A model that is useful in understanding how assumed motives influence behavior is shown below. It describes the power of **Assumed Motives.**

Assumed Motives

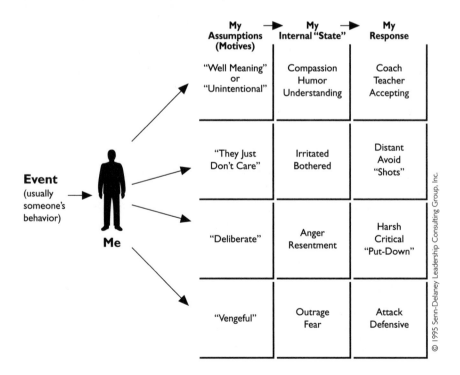

	My Assumptions (Motives)	My Internal "State"	My Response
	"Well Meaning" or "Unintentional"	Compassion Humor Understanding	Coach Teacher Accepting
Event (usually someone's behavior) → Me	"They Just Don't Care"	Irritated Bothered	Distant Avoid "Shots"
	"Deliberate"	Anger Resentment	Harsh Critical "Put-Down"
	"Vengeful"	Outrage Fear	Attack Defensive

We encourage those leading the reengineering effort to avoid assigning negative motives to the behavior of employees during times of change, and instead, see them through the eyes of compassion and understanding. By seeing the behavior as innocent reactions to fear and insecurity, it is easier to constructively engage in a healing dialogue that can assist those having the most difficulty get past their own insecurity and fears. The change management process calls forth real skills of understanding and compassion in those in leadership positions.

The best way for leaders to help employees caught up in resistance to change, is to be understanding and compassionate for the mental turmoil going on inside those individuals. Whenever employees exhibit counterproductive behavior, you can be certain they are in an insecure state of mind. If they were feeling more secure, they would see more of the opportunity and less of the fear associated with change. When leaders encounter resistance to change, they need to show extraordinary compassion, instead of resentment and defensiveness. They need to understand that otherwise excellent employees are just caught up in negative thoughts and resultant insecurities. Sometimes just maintaining your own sense of enthusiasm and well-being is enough to bring others to a higher level of thinking about the change process.

ESTABLISH STRONG REASONS FOR CHANGE... BOTH PERSONAL AND BUSINESS

The best advice for those leading a reengineering effort is to remember that "nothing happens until the sale is made!" In this case, the sale is the understanding and acceptance of the benefits of reengineering. We have noticed that all too often, senior management fully understands the need for and benefits of change, but then start down the road to change "assuming" that employees understand and see the same advantages. Too often, management does a very poor job of communicating the reasons for change. No wonder people tend to get frightened and resist.

While it may sound extreme, we suggest that the full implementation of reengineering shouldn't begin until most every employee, from the Chairman to the night janitor, understand the reason, the need, the imperative and the advantages for change. And this takes a focused communication campaign that is ongoing. One "all employee" meeting is not enough. It might be a good beginning, but we rather prefer the "water-drop" method of getting people's attention. Every internal publication, every staff meeting, every speech, every opportunity to tell the "story" for change should be taken. Special articles, as well as all internal publications should be filled with the "dangers of not changing" and the benefits and opportunities that are available if the organization embraces change.

Another excellent strategy for building the need for change is to describe not only what is happening in your own industry, but throughout the business world. Nothing is safe from global competition or quantum leaps in technology that may make your organization obsolete.

EXPECT SUCCESS

Leaders of reengineering must expect success. They should have a clear vision of what success means and confidently expect that those results will be delivered. When the leader confidently expects an objective to be met, people will tend to rise up to meet that expectation. Expecting success requires a high level of trust and respect in people. Leaders respect the abilities of their employees and trust that they will put forth their best efforts. In turn, employees respect the directions established by the leadership and trust that their efforts will be appreciated and fairly rewarded.

Success stories of how other companies have changed can help employees develop the necessary confidence for their own changes. "After all, if those guys could do it, so can we!" Leaders should talk about their confidence in the abilities and capabilities of employees. Paint a picture of what the end result will look like. Show everyone how we have the opportunity to create a responsive, "hassle-free" work environment for our customers and ourselves.

CELEBRATE THE "LITTLE WINS" ALL ALONG THE WAY

Reengineering success can be tremendous and far-reaching. But long before the big wins are realized, there are thousands of "little wins" that too often go unnoticed and most importantly, unappreciated. One of the keys to effective change management is to learn how to "celebrate along the way!" The old adage of "nothing succeeds like success" is very true during the often gut-wrenching process of reengineering.

Senior management and those leading the reengineering effort must learn how to seek out and openly appreciate the little wins, without which the bigger impact will not be gained.

In their landmark book on organizational change in the early 1980s, *In Search of Excellence*, Tom Peters and Robert Waterman stressed, in countless ways, the value of human celebration throughout the change process. We suggest you dig out your old copy and reread the section on "Productivity Through People" (pages 235–278). It contains some excellent and proven advice for how to really celebrate.

COACH THE "RESISTORS"

Occasionally, some people are so "gripped" with negative thoughts of fear and insecurity that they just can't get over it by themselves in the natural course of events as easily as others can. For now, let's call them our "resistors."

As the change process proceeds, your attention as the leader will keep coming back to the same set of individuals who just can't seem to get on with the change process. They keep asking the same questions about "why are we doing this?" They don't seem to listen to the benefits, but always keep coming up with the "yes, but..." responses as to why it's not going to work. And they tend to go around trying to enlist the support of other employees in resisting the change process.

At this stage there are really three approaches to take: Coach them; Reassign them; or Terminate them!

The coaching process is one of sitting down with them and truly listening to their concerns, fears, and points of view about the change process. In many cases, they just need to know that management has really heard their concerns. Think of this as the opportunity for them to get it "off their chest" that they didn't feel they had in a group setting. At this stage the leader's only job is to listen with compassion and understanding. And often, that's all it takes for these employees to move past their concerns and get on with the change process.

The next step in the coaching process is to again restate the situation the company is facing and the opportunity that reengineering offers. Then ask directly for their support and help. By asking, rather than demanding or threatening as in the old command-and-control leadership style, the choice becomes theirs alone, to finally support the process or not. More often than not, this step in the coaching process is the key to a behavior flip and a productive employee again.

If your coaching efforts fail, then an alternative is to reassign the individual to a part of the company, or another division, that will be less directly affected by the change process. Sometimes this is a good win-win outcome where the knowledge and talent of the individual can be retained, and the pathway cleared of resistance.

Termination is another way of eliminating those who can't get with the change process. While we believe this is a last resort, it is also a very powerful one that sends a definite signal throughout the organization that you are totally committed to the change process for the good of the organization as a whole. In our experience, it is not unusual for one or more senior officers to leave the organization during a reengineering process for lack of commitment and support for the changes required.

Reader Activity

Exploring Resistance

The following are some activities to do with your senior management team to help you better deal with the natural phenomenon of resistance during reengineering. As much as possible, we suggest you work out the responses and actions as a team. The discussion will be a great learning process in and of itself.

1. Establishing the Need for Change
   a. What are the external events in your industry and market place that are driving the need for change?

   b. What are the internal issues that make it necessary to implement change?

   c. List the benefits and opportunities from reengineering for—
   Customers:

   Employees:

2. List the numerous concerns and fears your employees may have about reengineering? (P.S. Don't forget to list *layoffs*!)

3. Develop a succinct, honest, and direct reply to each of the concerns listed above.

4. Identify your biggest current or potential "resistors."

5. What might be their fear, insecurity, or reason for resisting the reengineering process?

6. Who is going to be their "coach?" Assign each one a senior management "coach."

7. Who's in charge of celebrations? In what ways can we recognize and appreciate people for the little wins along the way?

12

CULTURAL CHOICE POINTS—WHAT TO DO WHEN

"We're talking about reengineering, but I don't know if it will really work here, or even if we really need it?"

"My boss has given me the assignment to fix our reporting cycle problems once and for all. How do I begin? And how do I avoid messing up this assignment?"

"We've just kicked off our Business Process Improvement efforts and already the teams are running into resistance, and we haven't even started changing things!"

"Boy are we stuck! It's been six months and we haven't even begun to see one dime of payback! And everyone, including me, is very discouraged."

These are very real statements and the feelings behind them are even more real; uncertainty, frustration, hopelessness, anger and resentment. It's not that the people or the process is flawed, its that in most cases these are the outcomes of the "Jaws of Culture" at work. These feelings surface when good people and needed improvements run into cultural barriers. In most cases, the choices made at these critical stages of the game will determine the success or failure of the improvement process.

No matter what size of business you run, what industry you are in, or where you are in the performance improvement process, you are probably facing some significant "choices." These choices revolve around the way culture either supports or hinders the change process. Some of the common "choice points" we have observed as well as some of the choices that support success include the following: *We're thinking about reengineering; We've just begun; We're well underway, but...; We're bogged down and it's not working; Pilot approach or do the entire company?;* and *Who should lead the reengineering process?*

WE'RE THINKING ABOUT REENGINEERING . . .

"And it came to pass that management spoke unto Human Resources saying, 'Behold thou shalt transfigure this company and launch it upon a Sea of Excellence!' And Human Resources spoke unto management saying, 'Are you sure you know what you are talking about?' "

One of the major choice points is whether or not to even begin a reengineering process. This is no small decision and one that should be considered very carefully.

One of the biggest questions must be answered first: Is senior management really ready to carry this process forward to success, to lead it, to allow it to grow and develop, to support the people and the process, and to be the real champions for change?

Even before the return on investment is calculated, or the reality of competitive pressures is factored in, senior management, especially the Chief Executive Officer, must come to grips with whether or not they will "go the distance." This choice is pivotal and should be decided early on. It is in part dependent upon a full understanding of what the time commitments and leadership commitments will be, as well as an understanding of the role that senior officers play in a massive change effort.

Some simple advice in this area may be helpful. If you have more time committed in your schedule for United Way Kick Offs and outside Board affiliations than you expect to devote to reengineering, don't start! You are not serious enough. Hopefully through this book you've realized that what we're really talking about is a culture-shift, not just improving a few key processes. That is a leadership function that cannot be delegated to a Steering Committee or a Reengineering Core Team.

If senior management fully understands the time and leadership commitment necessary, then the next choice is to determine whether or not it is really worth it.

The worksheet exercises in Chapter Two on the "Cost of Culture" and Chapter Five on "Building Objectives and Purpose," will help answer questions like:

- Will we get a big enough payoff to warrant embarking on this process?

- To what degree is our current culture acting as a barrier to the changes we need to make?

- Do we have the talent internally to place on the core team?

- Are we willing to give up our best people to populate these teams. (If not, don't even consider starting, because the word will quickly spread that the process really doesn't have the full commitment of management.)

WE'VE JUST BEGUN . . .

Even though you've chosen the reengineering consulting firm to work with, have formed the Steering Committee and the Reengineering Core Team, and begun the first phase of the process, it's not too late to begin a concurrent culture change process. In some cases the initial phases of the culture change process can be condensed and the necessary activities of culture change put into action to catch up with the initial stages of reengineering. A good example is our work at Washington Natural Gas in Seattle, Washington.

As the result of a referral from another natural gas client, we met with the Chairman of Washington Natural Gas and three of his senior managers. Washington Natural Gas is a 1,270-employee Natural Gas LDC in the Northwest. They had once been a highly profitable, diversified company, but through their own actions had gotten in trouble with the Public Utilities Commission and were "surprised" by a rate case refusal that led to serious financial difficulties. This was compounded because they were already spread thin with extensive diversification and aggressive marketing activities. As a result, a new CEO was brought in to revive the company, put it back on a solid financial footing, and prepare the organization for the coming deregulation of the natural gas industry.

Our initial meeting included the Senior VP of Legal, the Vice President of Human Resources, the Senior VP of Communications and the new CEO. When we began talking about the "Jaws of Culture" and the relationship between culture and reengineering, everyone perked up. We had a lively conversation about whether or not it was too late to work on the culture, since they had just chosen one of the Big Six Consulting Firms to be their reengineering partner. Could both reengineering and culture change be done simultaneously?

As a result of additional discussions, we began the culture change process with a Needs Assessment, followed quickly by a three-day off-site Leadership, Teambuilding, and Culture-Shaping workshop with the Reengineering Core Team, and a similar three-day off-site seminar with the Senior Executive Team a week later. The Core Team had spent six weeks doing their Process Mapping and they had already run into the "Jaws of Culture" and growing resistance. A first-ever corporate downsizing a few months earlier had left many of the employees with serious concerns and fears for their jobs and their future.

According to Keith Chrapczynski, Team Leader for the Reengineering Core Team at Washington Natural Gas, there were numerous cultural barriers that could easily have gotten in the way of their reengineering efforts:

> *"We recognized early in our reengineering effort that our likelihood of success could be dramatically improved by reshaping our corporate culture. As a management team, we knew we needed to reshape the old work environment, identify and break down the walls dividing individual departments, and nurture the rebuilding of relationships and personal commitment to the company as a whole."*

The initial culture change workshop was very well received and helped reshape a reengineering process into a fully integrated change and process improvement endeavor that blended both the activities of reengineering and culture change into a seamless set of activities that supported each other.

WE'RE BOGGED DOWN AND IT'S NOT WORKING

"That's it! I'm pulling the plug on all this. We've spent too much in time and effort and haven't gotten a single output, except reports and promises!"

This is perhaps the most difficult of all the "Choice Points" that must be faced in the life of a reengineering process. How does one make this choice correctly? Many of us hope that our situation is similar to the fellow who found "Acres of Diamonds" in his own backyard after years of digging and nearly giving up!

It's not a matter of there not being big potential rewards, it's really a matter of understanding how to achieve them with less wasted effort.

The examples of American Express and Amoco described earlier are good examples of what we believe is the best approach to this situation—pause, step back, reexamine the barriers though the lens of corporate culture, find the key levers to change, and recommit with 100% effort. Usually success is not far off. Sometimes it helps to remember that cultures have an incredible amount of "inertia" and it takes highly focused culture change activities to get the organization moving and embracing reengineering.

At Amoco, the third time was the charm. After reengineering failures in both 1986 and 1990, they were able to step back and look at the "unwritten" ground rules of the organization that were acting as cultural barriers to reengineering. In addition, they used the techniques of culture change, most notably getting employees involved through feedback and action teams. As a result, the process of reengineering the capital budgeting and planning processes yielded some big results in less time. According to John Carl, Amoco's EVP and Chief Financial Officer, the earlier problems stemmed from "not recognizing the interrelationship between management practices and processes."

PILOT APPROACH OR DO THE ENTIRE COMPANY?

The real question here is how broadly or narrowly do we start? Assuming the decision to embark on a reengineering effort has been well thought out and then made, it becomes a matter of resources, economics, and urgency!

There are two different approaches that can work equally well. If there is a serious time urgency to making dramatic improvement, a broad-based organization-wide effort is often necessary. This requires even more support from senior management and a concerted education and communications effort company-wide that conveys why "we're all about to change." When a compelling reason for change can be effectively communicated to the organization, and senior management is united in their support, then the clean sheet approach to the five to ten major organizational processes can be initiated simultaneously.

When more time is available and/or when more skepticism exists, it's useful to remember the power of the self-fulfilling prophecy and attempt to create what we call a "success wave." One example is work done by Senn-Delaney Leadership's former sister company, now a division of Arthur Andersen, that does operational consulting and reengineering in retailing. In working with one large multidivisional retailer, they began first with one division. They were able to help develop a process which moved goods from vendor to the selling floor in far less time with significantly less cost. Since the comparative numbers relative to other divisions were significantly better, it was easy to move the process into all divisions after that. In fact, as more divisions began to implement the process, a success wave based upon a positive self-fulfilling prophecy, was created and implementation became easy and quicker.

A pilot process or model store approach was used as a part of the turn-around of Montgomery Ward when it was threatened with extinction in the 80s. Since it wasn't possible to implement radical new methods and approaches in hundreds of stores all at once, model stores in different regions first took part in the process. When they achieved gains in sales and reductions in costs, skepticism was eliminated. In fact, the store managers of the model stores took part in a road show, in which the new approaches were rolled out to stores across the country with the model store managers showing the results and answering questions for their counterparts.

WHO SHOULD LEAD THE REENGINEERING PROCESS?

Most reengineering failures stem from breakdowns in leadership.

The real answer to this question is the CEO, President and Senior Team should lead the reengineering process. Without their full commitment and leadership the process will be crippled. There will come times when they will need to step forward and call the shots or confront the dissenters.

One of the informal ground rules we utilize in our work on culture change (and this should also apply to reengineering), is "let the leaders lead." In fact, any time the Steering Committee or Task Force gets out in front of the line leaders and begins to experience resistance they need to step back, work with the leaders and let them lead.

Since the President or CEO can't spend full time organizing and managing the effort, a second question exists: "Who should lead and organize the process?"

While "Leap Tall Buildings With a Single Bound" is often the most commonly thought of criteria for the Business Process Reengineering Champion or the Reengineering Process Head, that is too simplistic and narrow a view of the requirements (but sometimes useful!). The individual selected to head the reengineering effort obviously needs special capabilities and talents. But just what makes an effective reengineering leader?

We have found that successful leaders of reengineering come in all shapes, sizes, ages and from a wide variety of functions. However, overall they seem to have three characteristics in common:

- A *Clear Vision* of what the reengineered corporation can become.

- A fierce commitment to *Living-the-Values* of a high-performance culture.

- The *Courage* to take action.

One of the first questions asked of the new head of reengineering is "what does this reengineering look like when it's done?" The successful head of reengineering should have a clear picture of not only the processes, but be able to describe, in easy to understand terms that employees can relate to, the end state.

One of the first tasks of the individual chosen to head up the process should be to visit other companies who are far enough along in the reengineering process to provide a clear example of what results look like. During these field trips to other companies it is critical to meet with the Reengineering Team Leaders and the Head of the Reengineering process and talk with them openly about how to communicate the Vision, and the outcomes at the end of the process.

The successful Head of Reengineering must be a role model of the shared values and guiding behaviors of the new culture. They should be the "natural choice," the person whom everyone says: "That's the best person for the job, they really live the values, they really are committed to making a difference!" In addition, the process leader should be a facilitator, not an authoritarian; have good listening skills; and most of all, be open to new ideas, change, and letting others take the lead.

For example, in selecting Keith Chrapczynski as Team Leader for the Reengineering Core Team at Washington Natural Gas, the Senior Management Team and their consulting firm established four criteria in making their selection of who would be chosen to head up the reengineering effort. This criteria included the following key characteristics:

1. Has good project management skills.
2. Is an organizational risk-taker.
3. Has credibility within the organization.
4. Can create a high-performance team.

After looking at numerous possible candidates, Keith stood out on all the characteristics, plus he had a contagious sense of optimism that management felt would be needed as the process went along. They were right on all accounts!

Most of all, successful reengineering requires courage! The courage to take action, the courage to support a radical new idea or approach until it bears fruit, the courage to confront upper management when it is necessary, the courage to persist in spite of obstacles and setbacks.

In a recent article in *Fortune Magazine* ("What Team Leaders Need to Know"; February 20, 1995 pp. 93–100), the focus was on Team Leaders and how to win at this often confusing role. The article was built around a series of "Tips" for Team Leaders:

1. Don't be afraid to admit ignorance.
2. Know when to intervene.
3. Learn to truly share power.
4. Worry about what you take on, not what you give up.
5. Get used to learning on the job.

We add a 6th tip to this important list from our own observation of Team Leaders of Reengineering and Culture Change:

6. Have fun and make it fun for everyone!

In our experience, one of the best at this skill is Keith Chrapczynski at Washington Natural Gas.

From the onset, Keith has led his team with a great sense of humor and optimism. Although the work is very serious, the issues complex, and extremely stressful, Keith managed to interject the spirit of lighthearted fun into the environment. He held two teambuilding sessions for the Core Team with participant introductions being in the form of David Letterman's show—no one was able to take themselves too seriously on those days. For the Reengineering Core Team, every Wednesday is Pizza Day, and it is an open invitation for the various members of the Senior Management Team to drop by the Reengineering Offices and visit. As visitors to the Reengineering Offices walk the halls, besides the numerous flow charts of work processes and tracking diagrams, there are motivational posters, rubber snails stuck to the wall, humorous screen-savers, and hanging puppets, all of which indicate the spirit of creativity and "clean sheet" redesign that indicates that "something very special is going on around here."

While the Reengineering Leader can come from any part of the organization, there is one thing upon which most of our clients experienced in reengineering will agree; the leader should be someone with good business and people skills and not solely a technology person. Technology, particularly information systems, is a critical piece of the reengineering solution, but it is not the sole driver! The driver is the customer, not technology, and it is often a mistake to let technology lead the process. Find someone who is skilled in relating to the customer and who has a broad business outlook rather than a narrow functional specialty.

The Reengineering Core Team

No single person can accomplish radical business change. It takes all employees working together, often arranged in a series of teams: The Executive Steering Team, Reengineering Core Team, Process Diagnosis and Design Teams, Training Teams, Implementation Teams, and numerous others. Perhaps the most important of all the teams is the Reengineering Core Team.

Under the direction of the Head of Reengineering, the Core Team should be drawn from a cross-section of areas, functions, and levels in the company. While it is important to pick those individuals who are natural "change agents" and not stuck in the status quo, it is also important to have put several of the "older" employees on the team, and not just populate it with the young new thinkers. Adding the experience and wisdom of individuals who really know the business inside and out adds to the strength of the team, as well as the overall credibility of the team in the eyes of employees. Do not be afraid to seek out and recruit a few "critics," they often bring with them some good ideas and a real knowledge of the company's problems that haven't really been listened to before. It is also important to draw from middle management, since this is the area where the majority of job changes and layoffs tend to occur. This group will have some excellent insights into where and how retraining can take place, how to best communicate the personnel changes brought about by reengineering, and will also help the organization be sensitive to this important middle management group.

13

MAKING A DIFFERENCE— STAYING IN THE "EYE" OF THE STORM

We are in a period of unprecedented change that some liken to the magnitude of the Industrial Revolution. Organizations are having to reinvent themselves to be competitive. Business leaders are having to learn new skills to be effective. Employees are beginning to manage their own careers rather than expecting the company to do it for them. This translates into a myriad of simultaneous initiatives including: restructuring to better meet customer needs, bold competitive strategies, new information systems, customer satisfaction and quality initiatives and, of course, reengineering.

All of these initiatives are, to a greater or lesser degree, swimming against the tide of organizational habits we call "cultural barriers."

Nowhere can this be seen more clearly than in the breakthrough initiative of the 90s: Reengineering. True "clean sheet," cross-organizational reengineering by its very nature requires a healthy culture. All too often this is not the case. Real problems occur because Business Process Reengineering requires:

- Cross-organizational collaboration...when turf issues are common.
- Empowered employees...when hierarchy prevails.
- High levels of personal accountability...when people are feeling victimized, not accountable.
- Openness to change...when resistance is prevalent.
- Innovation and risk-taking...when a "bunker" mentality often creates risk aversion.

Not only are results diminished by dysfunctional cultures, but untold human prices are being paid by the ineffective implementation of reengineering. This takes the form of:

- massive layoffs instead of reengineered processes
- disenfranchised employees
- loss of loyalty, trust and commitment
- high levels of stress and burnout
- poor balance in life and neglected families

The answer to superior competitive performance and more fulfillment for people can be found in the qualities of a healthy culture and an enlightened, 21st Century style of leadership. In cultural terms, successful reengineering looks like:

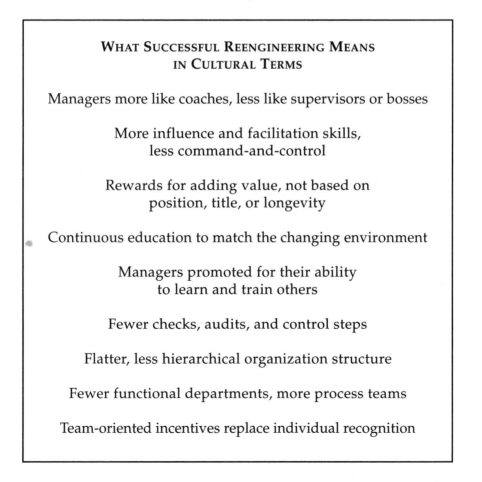

WHAT SUCCESSFUL REENGINEERING MEANS
IN CULTURAL TERMS

Managers more like coaches, less like supervisors or bosses

More influence and facilitation skills,
less command-and-control

Rewards for adding value, not based on
position, title, or longevity

Continuous education to match the changing environment

Managers promoted for their ability
to learn and train others

Fewer checks, audits, and control steps

Flatter, less hierarchical organization structure

Fewer functional departments, more process teams

Team-oriented incentives replace individual recognition

A MODEL FOR 21ST CENTURY LEADERSHIP

"During times of active change, everyone in the corporation has a leadership role, and an obligation to lead!"

—John Childress

We urge managers at all levels within organizations not to be a bystander nor a victim during these times of change. Whether or not your organization is actively addressing its cultural or leadership issues, **you can make a difference.** Everyone influences the culture around them, be it in their organization, their department, or their own work team. Each of us cast a shadow by our own behaviors and each of us has a choice in terms of our own personal and professional development.

In addition, organizational transformation does not take place without personal transformation. If everyone waits for those above them or around them to change, no one changes. This is the time when each individual needs to take a look at themselves and decide ways in which they need to change in order to more effectively deal with the changing times.

At the end of the year, many people make a list of New Year's resolutions to be more effective. As we approach the 21st Century, a new millennium, now is the time to begin to make resolutions on how to move toward becoming a 21st Century leader. We have developed a model of "personal paradigm shifts" to guide your journey.

A NEW MODEL FOR 21ST CENTURY LEADERSHIP

From Earlier Paradigm		*To Current and Future Paradigm*
Being a manager	⟾	Being a leader
Being a boss	⟾	Being a coach and facilitator
Controlling people	⟾	Empowering people
Holding on to authority	⟾	Delegating authority
Micro-managing	⟾	Leading with vision and values
Directing with rules and regulations	⟾	Guiding with winning shared values
Relying on "position power" and hierarchy	⟾	Building "relationship power" and networked teams
Demanding compliance	⟾	Gaining commitment
Focusing only on tasks	⟾	Focusing on quality, service and the customer
Confronting and combating	⟾	Collaborating and unifying
Going it alone	⟾	Utilizing the team
Judging others	⟾	Respecting, honoring and leveraging diversity and differences
Changing by necessity and crisis	⟾	Committing to continuous learning
Being internally competitive— (win/lose)	⟾	Being internally collaborative— (win/win)
Having a narrow focus, "me and my area"	⟾	Having a broader focus, "My team, my organization"

Final Thoughts on Reengineering

For those organizations and individuals embarking upon or engaged in reengineering, we would make the following recommendations:

- Get as committed to culture change as you are to the rewards of reengineering. Utilize change management processes and culture change trainings to simultaneously address leadership skills, teambuilding, and culture change.

- Engage in reengineering and culture change concurrently to maximize efficiency and provide synergy—they will support one another.

- Don't start unless you're serious. Starting and stopping creates incredible frustration and alienation among employees.

- Don't quit, even if it looks like things are not working. Usually it's just a need to be persistent and make certain you are getting everyone involved in the process.

- Counsel your resistors, in or out—especially those among senior management. There is no room for spectators in the process of reengineering and culture change.

- Communicate—Appreciate—Communicate.

- Celebrate the little wins along the way.

- Laugh (a lot); it's therapeutic for everyone!

Final Thoughts on Culture

All that you do or attempt to do in your organization will be influenced by your culture. Therefore, you might want to keep the following in mind:

- Your organization has a culture whether you want it to or not.

- The only choice you have is whether you proactively influence it or not.

- Cultures can be "reengineered" just like processes can. It just takes a different technology to do it.

- Whether you lead a company, a department, or a team, you influence the culture of that group by the shadow you cast. "Who you are and how you behave speaks louder than any words you use."

- A healthy, high-performance culture is the greatest asset an organization or team can have.

- Even though these are turbulent times, you can operate from the calm *in the eye of the storm* if your organization has a healthy culture and you maintain a healthy state of mind.

ABOUT THE AUTHORS

John Childress and Larry Senn co-founded the Senn-Delaney Leadership Consulting Group, Inc. in 1978 with the vision of *"Making a Difference Through Leadership."* The professionals at Senn-Delaney Leadership coach and consult with CEOs and the senior management teams of corporations around the world on reshaping corporate culture, teambuilding, empowerment, quality, service and leadership development. Their innovative custom-tailored seminars and consulting engagements have been utilized by CEOs to bring about lasting organizational change and business improvement.

Prior to *"In the Eye of the Storm: Reengineering Corporate Culture,"* John and Larry have collaborated on two other books on business leadership, teambuilding and culture change issues, *"21st Century Leadership: Dialogues with 100 Top Leaders"* (with Lynne Joy McFarland), and a workbook and reference manual on *"Leadership, Teambuilding, and Culture Change"* (with Bernadette Senn).

JOHN R. CHILDRESS

John is President and CEO of the Senn-Delaney Leadership Consulting Group, Inc. John has a master's degree from Harvard and over 20 years of experience in business consulting, focusing specifically on executive coaching, change management, and leadership development.

John's distinctive competence is working with CEOs on aligning senior teams around new strategies and structures and assisting them in shaping cultures to support specific initiatives, including reengineering.

An accomplished group facilitator and coach, John effectively brings to life for clients the issues of leadership, teamwork and personal development. John addresses many organizations each year to discuss leadership and the importance of culture change issues.

John and his family live in Carmel, California.

LARRY E. SENN

Dr. Larry Senn is Chairman of the Senn-Delaney Leadership Consulting Group. He is a pioneer in the area of Corporate Culture. In the mid-60s, while working on his doctoral dissertation, Larry conducted the first systematic field study of how corporate culture impacts success in corporations.

Prior to founding Senn-Delaney Leadership, Larry had co-founded Senn-Delaney Management Consultants with Jim Delaney. The original firm focused on productivity improvement/reengineering. The challenges encountered in trying to implement change in dysfunctional cultures led to the formation of the Leadership Consulting Group. Senn-Delaney Management Consultants is now a part of the Arthur Andersen Operations Consulting Practice. The Leadership Consulting Group remains a private partner-owned firm.

For almost 20 years Larry has worked with Fortune 1000 leaders to transform their organizations. Whether coaching CEOs one-on-one, or facilitating a session in front of a room of 30 or 1,000 people, Larry is a masterful facilitator and speaker. He has served as a member of the team that designed the first White House Quality/Service Summit, and has appeared on numerous television and business shows, including PBS and the CBS American Business Journal.

Larry and his family live in Sunset Beach, California.

ABOUT SENN-DELANEY LEADERSHIP

Senn-Delaney Leadership employs a diverse group of consulting professionals with broad business backgrounds and expertise in cultural transformation, the management of change, teambuilding, organizational effectiveness, and leadership development. They assess, customize and implement leadership consulting engagements for major corporations in the U.S. and around the world.

Senn-Delaney Leadership Consulting Group has worked with hundreds of leaders and their teams on the following kinds of engagements:

- Broad-based culture change initiatives designed to promote values including: openness to change, empowerment, accountability, teamwork, trust and a bias for action.

- Creation of organizational behaviors needed to successfully implement initiatives including: Total Quality, customer service, restructuring, reengineering, or new strategies.

- Executive teambuilding and the creation of high-performance teams to better lead organizations.

- Assistance in creating a compelling vision and/or aligning the organization around it.

- Teambuilding to more quickly bring together restructured teams or teams with a new leader.

- Assistance to overcome "culture clash" common in mergers and negotiations.

- Design of Comprehensive Change Management strategies for organizations.

- Leadership development processes, including one-on-one executive coaching and use of customized 360° feedback instruments.

For additional information about the consulting services of Senn-Delaney Leadership, please contact us at our corporate headquarters:

Senn-Delaney Leadership Consulting Group, Inc.
3780 Kilroy Airport Way
Long Beach, California 90806
Phone (310) 426-5400
Fax (310) 426-5174

REFERENCE LIST

INTRODUCTION: A STORM IS RAGING

Stewart, Thomas. Reengineering—The Hot New Managing Tool. *Fortune*, Aug. 23, 1993.

Hammer, Michael, and Champy, James. *Reengineering the Corporation—A Manifesto for Business Revolution*. Harper Business Press, 1993.

Champy, James. *Reengineering Management—The Mandate for New Leadership*. Harper Business Press, 1995.

Smith, Ray, Chairman and Chief Executive Officer, Bell Atlantic Corporation. Personal interview, 1992.

Morris, Brenda, Director of Reengineering, Bell Atlantic Corporation. Personal interview, Feb., 1995.

Wellins, Richard S. and Murphy, Julie Schulz. Reengineering: Plug into the Human Factor. *Training and Development*, January, 1995.

1 REENGINEERING: AN OPPORTUNITY FOR REAL CHANGE

Corporate reduction figures on page 21 were obtained at the Hammer Reengineering Conference, "The Reengineered Corporation: Reinventing the Systems of Management." Oct. 31–Nov. 2, 1994, Boston, Massachusetts.

CSC Index, Inc., State of Reengineering Report (North America and Europe), 1994. Pioneer consulting firm in reengineering conducted study of twenty recent case studies.

Musone, Fred, Federal Mogul Corporation. Personal interview, Feb., 1995, and information at the Hammer Reengineering Conference, "The Reengineered Corporation: Reinventing the Systems of Management." Oct. 31–Nov. 2, 1994, Boston, Massachusetts.

Karlgaard, Rich, ASAP Interview with Mike Hammer, *Forbes Magazine*, 1994.

Stewart, Thomas. Reengineering. The Hot New Managing Tool. *Fortune*, August 23, 1993.

Pepsi. Information and case study obtained at the Hammer Reengineering Conference, "The Reengineered Corporation: Reinventing the Systems of Management." Oct. 31–Nov. 2, 1994, Boston, Massachusetts.

McFarland, Lynne Joy, Senn, Larry E., and Childress, John R. *21st Century Leadership—Dialogues with 100 Top Leaders*. The Leadership Press, Inc., 1993.

Business Intelligence. *Reengineering: The Critical Success Factors*. A Management Special Report, Management Publications Limited, London, England, 1994.

Tom Peters and the Healthy Organization. *Psychology Today*, March/April 1993.

2 STORM CLOUDS: THE PROBLEMS ARE BIGGER THAN WE THOUGHT

CSC Index, Inc. State of Reengineering Report (North America and Europe), 1994.

Arthur D. Little. Survey cited in *Informationweek* article by Caldwell, Bruce. Missteps, Miscues. *Informationweek*, June 20, 1994.

McKinsey and Company. Cited in Gross, Tracy, Pascale, Richard, and Athos, Anthony. The Reinvention Roller Coaster: Risking the Present for a Powerful Future. *Harvard Business Review*, Nov.–Dec., 1993.

Deloitte & Touche, survey cited in Caldwell, Bruce. Missteps, Miscues. Article in *Informationweek*, June 20, 1994.

Welch, Jack, Chairman and Chief Executive Officer, General Electric. Personal interview, 1993. For the book, *21st Century Leadership—Dialogues with 100 Top Leaders*.

Christofferson, Randy, Senior Vice President of quality and reengineering, American Express. Speech at the Hammer Reengineering Conference, "The Reengineered Corporation: Reinventing the Systems of Management." Oct. 31–Nov. 2, 1994, Boston, Massachusetts.

Carl, John, Executive Vice President and Chief Financial Officer, Amoco Corporation. Speech at the Hammer Reengineering Conference, "The Reengineered Corporation: Reinventing the Systems of Management." Oct. 31–Nov. 2, 1994, Boston, Massachusetts.

CSC Index, Inc., State of Reengineering Report (North America and Europe), 1994.

Gross, Tracy, Pascale, Richard, and Athos, Anthony. The Reinvention Roller Coaster: Risking the Present for a Powerful Future. *Harvard Business Review*, Nov.–Dec., 1993.

Croom, John, Chief Executive Officer, Columbia Gas Systems. Personal interview, 1995.

Wallingford, Logan W., Senior Vice President, Columbia Gas System. Personal interview, May 1995.

Casdorph, Mike, Senior Vice President, Columbia Gas Transmission. Personal interview, 1995.

Caldwell, Bruce. Missteps, Miscues. *Informationweek*, June 20, 1994.

3 CHARTING A NEW COURSE: REENGINEERING, LEADERSHIP AND CULTURE CHANGE

Markus, Lynne, Associate Professor of Information Science at Claremont Graduate School. Adapted from Blood, Sweat and Tears. *Informationweek*, June 20, 1994.

Yount, Michael, Transcontinental Gas Pipeline Company. Personal interview, April, 1995.

Schein, Edgar. *How Culture Forms, Develops and Changes*. Jossey-Bass, 1985.

McFarland, Lynne Joy, Senn, Larry E., and Childress, John R. *21st Century Leadership—Dialogues with 100 Top Leaders*. The Leadership Press, Inc., 1993.

Welch, Jack, Chairman and Chief Executive Officer, General Electric. Personal interview, 1993. For the book, *21st Century Leadership—Dialogues with 100 Top Leaders*.

Turnstall, W. Brooke. *Disconnected Parties*. McGraw-Hill Book Company, 1985.

4 LINKING REENGINEERING AND CULTURE CHANGE

Musone, Fred, Federal Mogul Corporation. Personal interview at the Hammer Reengineering Conference, "The Reengineered Corporation: Reinventing the Systems of Management." Oct. 31–Nov. 2, 1994, Boston, Massachusetts.

Senn, Larry E., *Organizational Character as a Tool in the Analysis of Business Organizations*, Unpublished doctoral dissertation, University of Southern California, Los Angeles, CA, 1970.

Senn-Delaney Leadership Consulting Group, Inc. From *Culture Change Process Model* of leadership training seminar, Long Beach, CA, 1995.

Arthur Andersen LLP, *A Business Process Reengineering Model*, New York, NY, 1995.

5 PHASE I: STRATEGIC UNDERSTANDING OF CULTURE CHANGE

Kotter, John P. and Heskett, James L. *Corporate Culture and Performance*, The Free Press, 1992.

Deal, Terrence E. and Kennedy, Allen A. *Corporate Cultures: The Rites and Rituals of Corporate Life*. Addison-Wesley, 1982.

Burke, James, Former Chairman, Johnson and Johnson. Personal interview and Press Kit Materials, 1993. For the book, *21st Century Leadership—Dialogues with 100 Top Leaders*.

Welch, Jack, Chairman and Chief Executive Officer, General Electric. Personal interview, 1993. For the book, *21st Century Leadership—Dialogues with 100 Top Leaders*.

Iacocca, Lee, Former Chairman and Chief Executive Officer, Chrysler. Personal interview, 1993. For the book, *21st Century Leadership—Dialogues with 100 Top Leaders.*

Executive Leadership Workshops conducted by Senn-Delaney Leadership Consulting Group, Inc.

Murfitt, Maggie, Rank Xerox UK, personal interview and speech at the Hammer Reengineering Conference, "The Reengineered Corporation: Reinventing the Systems of Management." Oct. 31–Nov. 2, 1994, Boston, Massachusetts.

Allison, John, Chairman of Branch Banking & Trust Company (BB&T), personal interview by Arthur Andersen LLP, April, 1995.

6 PHASE II: CORPORATE CULTURE AUDIT
Three-Day Off-Site Senior Retreat conducted by Senn-Delaney Leadership Consulting Group, Inc.

Casdorph, Mike, Senior Vice President, Columbia Gas Transmission. Personal interview, 1995.

Corporate Culture Profile℠, 1995 by Senn-Delaney Leadership Consulting Group, Inc., Long Beach, CA.

7 PHASE III: BEGIN AT THE TOP
Gault, Stanley, Chairman, Goodyear Tire and Rubber. Personal interview with Jacqueline M. Graves for *Fortune* article, Corporate Change, Dec. 14, 1992.

Graves, Jacqueline M. Leaders of Corporate Change. *Fortune,* Dec. 14, 1992.

Nolte, Dorothy Law. *Children Learn What They Live.* Ross Laboratories. Living Scrolls, 1972.

Deakins, Warren, President and Chief Executive Officer, Fidelity Mutual Life Insurance Company. Personal interview, 1993. For the book, *21st Century Leadership—Dialogues with 100 Top Leaders.*

Blanchard, Marjorie M., President, Blanchard Training and Development, Inc. Personal interview, 1993. For the book, *21st Century Leadership—Dialogues with 100 Top Leaders.*

Houghton, Jamie, Chief Executive Officer, Corning, Inc. Personal interview by Arthur Anderson LLP, May, 1995.

Morehouse, Alice, Vice President of Operations, Blue Cross and Blue Shield of the National Capital Area. Personal interview by Arthur Anderson LLP, May, 1995.

Smith, Ray, Chairman and Chief Executive Officer, Bell Atlantic Corporation. Personal interview with Larry Senn, 1992.

Hall, Eugene A., Rosenthal, James, and Wade, Judy. How to Make Reengineering Really Work. *The McKinsey Quarterly,* 1994, Number 2.

8 PHASE IV: DESIGNING A HIGH-PERFORMANCE CULTURE

Kotter, John P. and Heskett, James L. *Corporate Culture and Performance.* The Free Press, 1992.

Welch, Jack, Chairman and Chief Executive Officer, GE. Personal interview, 1993. For the book, *21st Century Leadership—Dialogues with 100 Top Leaders.*

Scotese, Peter, retired Chief Executive Officer, Spring Industries. Personal interview, 1993. For the book, *21st Century Leadership—Dialogues with 100 Top Leaders.*

McFarland, Lynne Joy, Senn, Larry E., and Childress, John R. *21st Century Leadership—Dialogues with 100 Top Leaders.* The Leadership Press, Inc., 1993.

Kearns, David, Former Chairman and Chief Executive Officer, Xerox. Personal interview, 1993. For the book, *21st Century Leadership—Dialogues with 100 Top Leaders.*

Macomber, John D., Former Chairman and President, Export-Import Bank of the United States. Personal interview, 1993. For the book, *21st Century Leadership—Dialogues with 100 Top Leaders.*

Burke, James, Former Chairman, Johnson and Johnson. Personal interview, 1993. For the book, *21st Century Leadership—Dialogues with 100 Top Leaders.*

Allison, John, Chairman, BB&T Financial. Speech delivered at the Hammer Reengineering Conference, "The Reengineered Corporation: Reinventing the Systems of Management." Oct. 31–Nov. 2, 1994, Boston, Massachusetts.

Katzenbach, Jon, and Smith, Doug, of McKinsey and Company, *The Wisdom of Teams.* Harper Business Press, 1994.

Peters, Thomas J., and Waterman, Robert H. *In Search of Excellence.* Harper and Row, 1982.

Mosbacher, Georgette. *Feminine Force—Release the Power Within to Create the Life You Deserve.* Simon and Shuster, 1993.

Sykes, Charles J. *A Nation of Victims.* St. Martin's Press, 1992.

Niebuhr, Reinhold, Theologian and author of The Serenity Prayer.

Gates, Bill, Chief Executive Officer, Microsoft Corporation. Personal interview, 1993. For the book, *21st Century Leadership—Dialogues with 100 Top Leaders.*

Kipper, Barbara Levy, Chairman, Chas. Levy Company. Personal interview, 1993. For the book, *21st Century Leadership—Dialogues with 100 Top Leaders.*

Healy, Bernadine, Director, National Institutes of Health. Personal interview, 1993. For the book, *21st Century Leadership—Dialogues with 100 Top Leaders.*

Maurer, Rick. *Caught in the Middle.* Productivity Press, 1992.

Pepper, John, President, Procter & Gamble Company. Personal interview, 1993. For the book, *21st Century Leadership—Dialogues with 100 Top Leaders.*

General Electric Power Generation. Personal interview by Arthur Anderson LLP, May, 1995. Used with permission.